Vulnerable but Invincible

MEMOIRS OF A SINGAPORE DOCTOR IN AUSTRALIA

Bernice Eu

For all those who are vulnerable but invincible...

Bernice Eu, 2022

Vulnerable but Invincible

MEMOIRS OF A SINGAPORE DOCTOR
IN AUSTRALIA

Bernice Eu

DoctorZed
Publishing
www.doctorzed.com

Copyright © 2022 by Bernice Eu

All rights reserved. No part of this book may be used or reproduced by any means, graphic, electronic, or mechanical, including photocopying, recording, taping or by any information storage retrieval system without the written permission of the publisher except in the case of brief quotations embodied in critical articles and reviews.

All the stories contained within are true, but some of the locations and people's names have been changed.

First published 2022 by DoctorZed Publishing.

DoctorZed Publishing books may be ordered through booksellers or by contacting:

DoctorZed Publishing
IDAHO
10 Vista Ave
Skye, South Australia 5072
www.doctorzed.com
info@doctorzed.com

ISBN: 978-0-6455705-9-5 (hc)
ISBN: 978-0-6455442-0-6 (sc)
ISBN: 978-0-6455442-1-3 (e)

A CIP number for this book is available at the National Library of Australia. This is a work of non-fiction. The views expressed in this work are solely those of the author and do not necessarily reflect the views of the publisher, and the publisher hereby disclaims any responsibility for them.

DoctorZed Publishing rev. date: 22/09/2022

To my family.

ACKNOWLEDGEMENTS

I thank those who have urged me to write my memoir, in the face of my advancing years. Some of these are:

May, a close family friend whose can-do attitude sped this memoir forward.

Brenda, my friend, who was taken away too soon, and who sent me these words: "The world needs your voice, your good heart, your belief in what can be. The world needs you just as you are."

Rob, my son, who gave me a thesaurus and wrote:
"Dearest Nana,
May inspiration abound
And your words flow like water."

Angus, my grandson, said: "Nana, you are a legend."
I said: "Only dead people are legends."
He said: "Well, you are a living legend."

Scarlett, my granddaughter, said, when giving a speech on the best age to be: "...I'd like being 80 years old, like my Nana... She is like Barbie, she is a doctor, a politician and now that she is retired, she is writing a book..."

Sophie, my older granddaughter: "She just cares."

Laurence, my brother, was an avid watcher and photographer of birds around Singapore and Australia.

I was taken with his tale of a certain bird called the dark-shouldered kite. Laurence was out bird watching when he came across a dark-shouldered kite whose wing was tangled in the branch of a tree. He took a photo of the distressed bird and then untangled its wing.

The bird promptly flew away. My brother continued bird watching, but when he returned later that day to the spot where he had freed the bird, there was the bird looking at him. Laurence took a photo and they continued to look at each other in silence. The bird then flew away.

When I asked Laurence if I could use his two photos of the dark-shouldered kite for my memoirs, he was very chuffed. I am now extra-pleased to use his photographs of the bird on the cover of this book as my brother has since passed away.

'Vulnerable but Invincible' was the term coined by E. E. Werner to describe premature children and their struggles.

CONTENTS

Chapter 1 – Arrival	9
Chapter 2 – Vulnerable but Invincible	16
Chapter 3 – University Days	32
Chapter 4 – Woomera Detention Centre	42
Chapter 5 – War Zone in South Australia	52
Chapter 6 – Medical Internship & Further Medical Skills	57
Chapter 7 – Singapore & Family	64
Chapter 8 – Love	85
Chapter 9 – A Refugee	95
Chapter 10 – Politics	106
Epilogue	120

CHAPTER 1

Arrival

I am alone.

The four-hour drive from Adelaide to the rural town of Woomera has put more than just miles behind me. I've left behind everything that is safe, comfortable, and familiar—my husband, my home and my position as a Member of the South Australian Parliament. It is December 1999.

With just a few short weeks until the new millennium, it seems to be the perfect time for a fresh start—although there is nothing fresh about Woomera on this searingly hot, parchment dry December day. The intense blue, cloudless sky provides an unchanging backdrop to the immense, flat-to-the-horizon car park of Woomera Detention Centre. I reluctantly emerge from the cool of my air-conditioned car into the forty-four degree heat, and am instantly hit by a gust of wind that brings dust to my throat and eyes, choking and blinding me. My vision clears, to reveal the stunted trees that sparsely dot the barren landscape, and the clunky outline of Woomera Detention Centre, fenced all around with twelve-foot-high chain-linked metal, topped with coils of razor-sharp barbed wire that flash dangerously in the morning sun.

I walk towards the checkpoint, staffed by two guards, with another three nearby. As they see me, they stop talking abruptly. One of the guards speaks.

"Who are you?"

I bristle at the unnecessary hostility, wondering if it's because I'm a woman, or because I'm Asian or because he just speaks to everyone like that. I reach into my bag for my mobile phone so that I can check the date I'm supposed to arrive, in case I have made a mistake.

"No mobile phones allowed. You'll have to leave that here," the guard continues, with the same charmless tone.

"I'm the new medical doctor. I need my phone for safety, and for medical communication…"

"No need. Plenty of phones inside. Rules are rules," he cuts me off.

"Just call Tony. Tony Hamilton-Smith. I'm sure he will allow…"

"No. He's in a meeting," the guard cuts in again.

Pulling myself up to my full five-foot, I grip my phone and stride past the guards, desperately holding on to my ebbing nerves as I push through the doors and into the administration office, where a middle-aged, sour-faced woman sits behind the front counter.

"Where is Tony?" I ask urgently.

The woman glances up briefly. "In a meeting," she drawls dismissively, jabbing her finger towards a door nearby.

"And who are you?" she says, echoing the guard's charmless tone.

"I'm the new doctor."

The now red-faced receptionist jumps up to show me the way. I walk past, ignoring her, and barge into the meeting room.

Five faces turn in unison. Four of them are visibly annoyed, but to my relief, the fifth face smiles with recognition in his eyes; it is Anthony Hamilton-Smith, the manager of the Department of Immigration and Multicultural and Indigenous Affairs.

"Hello, Bernice, I was wondering when you'd be arriving. Let me introduce you to everyone."

Tony runs through the names and roles of each of the managers, and I promptly forget them.

I tell him what happened with the guards, and he immediately agrees that I should keep my mobile phone with me. He then excuses himself from the meeting and takes me to the medical centre.

The medical centre, although larger than the administration centre, is similar to the row-upon-row of grey box-like structures known as 'dongas' that form the accommodation for the asylum seekers. The dongas remind me of the lyrics to a Pete Seeger song, "Little boxes made of ticky-tacky, and they all look just the same."

The medical centre consisted of two small consulting rooms—the doctor's consulting room was just big enough to fit an examination couch, a desk and chair, a filing cabinet and two chairs for the patient and a guard. The other examination room was even smaller. The other main area of the medical centre was not much larger than each of the two consulting rooms, and was used by the four registered nurses who worked at the centre for storing medication and equipment, sorting laboratory results, making appointments and writing reports. Finally, there was the 'waiting room', which was little more than a passageway, where the patients sat, accompanied by their guard, until their name was called.

When the nurses tell me that there are 1,000 adult asylum seekers and 200 children in the centre, I think to myself, *The medical centre seems woefully inadequate for the services it has to provide. How will I work in such cramped conditions?*

I open my mouth to vocalise my thoughts when there's a *bang! bang! bang!* on the door of the centre.

I shut my mouth. Before anyone can get to the door, it's flung open by two hefty guards, dragging and hauling a struggling man shouting what I can only surmise are unpleasant invectives.

The guards scream back, "Just shut the fuck up!"

They drag the man into the smaller consulting room and fling him onto the examination couch. He crawls as far away from them as possible, huddling in the corner of the couch, still shouting aggressively and waving his arms wildly to keep himself free from the grip of the guards.

"You stay there, or else!" shouts a guard, showing a fist about to strike, to illustrate what 'else' was going to be.

I steel myself, visually searching the patient in front of me for some clue to account for his behaviour.

I see a man of medium height and weight crouched in the corner of the couch, not cowering, but defiant. His eyes are wide-open, bulging with rebellion, looking straight at me. His hair is dark, and he's clean-shaven—unlike most of the Middle Eastern asylum seekers I will soon meet. He is sturdy and tough, and yet his hands are clean. He now moves more gently.

He is not going to spring on me

"Look, Doc, this guy—Pok 63—is a big troublemaker. You need to do something!"

I ignore the guard and address the man.

"What do you want?"

"Nothing," he replies in English.

"Well, if you behave like this, you will make yourself sick!" I shrug.

"Want sick. I want to die! Inshallah"—*God willing*, he replies in a belligerent tone.

If you have an unexpected visitor that you don't like, then offer him a drink rather than show your exasperation, I think to myself, grateful for the wisdom of my Chinese culture.

"Would you like a drink?"

"Yes."

"Some water?"

"Coca Cola!" he barks back.

The two guards gasp, "Doc, he's fucking with you! Even we don't get Coke!"

"Just get him a Coke," I say crisply.

"But…but…" they sputter incredulously.

"Who is the doctor here?" I ask.

With copious swearing and numerous threats to the patient, they proceed to get the offensive Coke.

I look around the centre to find Tony or one of the nurses, but with no luck. I am not aware of when they left, but I feel isolated.

What…? They left me in this risky situation!! Does this happen often? What have I signed up for? It's certainly not like my usual general practice!

I ask the patient what his name is.

"Oday," he replies, "but they call me Pok 63."

"Why?" I ask, bemused.

"No one call by our names. We call by boat name. My boat was called Pok, and I number 63,"—accompanied with a shrug of his shoulder.

I found this method unacceptable and queried the management about it at the earliest opportunity. Their reply was that most of the asylum seekers were called Mohammed, and it was too confusing. When I argued that there were other names attached to Mohammed, they complained that the other names were too difficult to pronounce! I could not accept the practice, and refused to call anyone by the name of a boat. I pressed the management on this matter continually, until the practice was discontinued.

When the Coke arrived, Oday took the can, sipped the liquid and smiled at me. When he had calmed down, I coaxed him to tell his story.

He tells me his full name is Oday Al-Tikriti. He comes from the town of Tikrit—Saddam Hussein's hometown. Oday's father was a minister under the Saddam regime, but he did not see eye to eye with Saddam's policies nor his methods. In the end, Oday's father was poisoned by Saddam. As Oday tells me this, his face is etched with profound grief, and he is unable to control his weeping. He tells me that after his father's murder it was not safe for him in Iraq anymore, so he fled, leaving his wife, mother, three sisters, a brother and their families in Baghdad.

Oday had arrived at the Woomera Detention Centre just days before me, after making his way overland, and then by boat to Indonesia, where he waited for a month, before finally getting onto an overcrowded boat for Australia. It was so crowded that the rats had to jump over the humans to find a space for themselves.

Oday explains that it had been difficult for him to stay in contact with his wife during his journey to Australia, and that when he was finally permitted a phone call from the detention centre, she told him that she was leaving him.

I decide to counsel him two to three times a week, as a precautionary measure to monitor deterioration in his mental health and to prevent further incidents.

With this care plan in place, the destructive behaviour quickly stopped.

As Oday spoke relatively good English compared to many of the other Middle Eastern detainees, when the two overworked translators were not available, he would step in. Sometimes this meant getting up at 3am. When he wasn't translating, he would spend his days walking endlessly around the barbed wire perimeter; waiting, waiting, desperate to know when he would be released.

How could he have known that it would not be weeks, nor months, but years before that time comes.

CHAPTER 2
Vulnerable but Invincible

I am alone.

It is late afternoon, in early September 2021. I lie back on the bed in my Sydney hotel room, under quarantine for fourteen days after returning from a compassionate visit to Singapore.

In the mornings, the sun beats down on my bed. In the afternoon it moves round to the back window, where my bathroom is situated. Since when am I interested in the rotation of the sun? I ache to be released, but as I wait, my thoughts drift back over the years. I think firstly of Woomera. I try to imagine what it must have been like for Oday and the other asylum seekers at the detention centre—two weeks' quarantine seems interminable. What must it have been like to be locked up indefinitely?

I think how different my own experience of first arriving in Australia had been from that of the people at Woomera. My mind travels back further, to the place I have just returned from, the place of my birth—Singapore—with its beautiful scenes of overwhelming greenery and colourful orchids, frangipani, bougainvillea and soft breezes that drift across the hot and humid tropical island.

I think about the food, about those hidden places where you can get the best Nonya food, the best lobster noodle, the best roast pork and the best Indian rojak on the whole island. I breathe deeply with the memory of the intoxicating aroma.

I recall when my daughter was about twelve, I took her to Singapore. There, she unexpectedly asked me, "Mum, why do all your family always talk about food? You guys live to eat, not eat to live." I was taken aback, but on further thought, I understood.

And so, I shall take this opportunity to reflect on why we Asians seem to incessantly talk about food!

The first time my husband, John, came with me to Singapore he was invited to a banquet given by my most senior relative, Ah Kong, at his tiered-cake mansion in Cairnhill Circle, Singapore. Ee Kim Poh—a title denoting a grand aunt married to a second son—was to look after him at the banquet.

There were about fifteen courses, all of which John had to navigate with unfamiliar chopsticks. He did well. However, with each delicious course he finished, Ee Kim Poh would refill his bowl for a second serve. This happened with several courses. He covered his bowl with his hand indicating 'no more' but to no avail, as his hand was brushed away. He nudged me, and I thought it was a nudge of approval, and that he was loving the food!

Ee Kim Poh then said in her best English, nodding her head and beaming, "Your husband like food, he eat, all finish. I give him more." John shook his head. I then whispered that if he didn't want more, he had to leave a little food in his bowl. From that moment on, magically, he had one serve only for each course! He looked extremely relieved!

I have always been fond of good food. In particular, hawker food and Nonya food. The hawkers had a long, strong, flexible wooden pole, from which hung two large, covered buckets, one at each end of the pole. They would carry these buckets by shouldering the middle of the pole and lifting up the whole device. When a hawker arrived at his roadside position, he would lower his load, steady his buckets on the ground, remove the pole and take out a little stool. He would then sit on the stool and begin to arrange his food for sale. His food was usually nuts and beans, sold in newspaper twisted into cones, filled to the top with the lovely, golden, crispy delicacies.

Other hawkers sold rice with vegetable or meat dishes. The better-off hawkers had tricycles with a large square receptacle on the front, serving as a cooker, with which he could fry noodles, cook soups and bake Nonya cupcakes. We waited for these hawkers as they swung by our houses, calling out their wares and knocking out a rhythm with two bamboo stick. They would each knock out a particular rhythm, and with each different rhythm we would know who was coming by and what he was selling—similar to an ice-cream van driving down the street with its special melody.

These hawkers are few and far between nowadays. They are now located in food courts all over Singapore's suburbs. Some food courts are air-conditioned, but the more basic food courts have fans, with long stone tables and benches that seat up to a dozen people.

Food court meals consist of breakfast of toast with a Nonya jam known as 'kaya', accompanied by strong, black coffee. Kaya is made with eggs, coconut milk and caramel sugar, all infused with a strong aromatic leaf called the pandan leaf. My second grandmother would make kaya, stirring and stirring and stirring it over a low flame until the jam was silky, thick and aromatic. As a child, I would sit with my second grandmother at my Ah

Kong's mansion as she stirred, then I'd hop on my bike and ride around the grounds before going back to her, still sitting and stirring. I used to ask her if I could help stir and she would reply in Cantonese, "You go away. You can't even sit for two minutes," before giving me a small smack on my bottom and shooing me away.

The other hawker breakfast is the rice porridge, known as 'chok'. There are two items that make the best chok. The rice porridge itself must be cooked to a certain consistency, so that the grains of rice hold their shape but melt in your mouth when eaten. You then nominate the flavour by choosing a meat, fish or vegetable to be added. These ingredients must be very fresh and of top quality. My favourite is fish, known as 'Ikan Tenggeri'—mackerel, finely sliced with ginger and garlic.

Lunch is gourmet hour in the food court, with each stall specialising in their own particular dishes and no one stall like another.

For dinner, the restaurants were the focus, rather than the food halls. Here, we had fine French and Italian cuisine, alongside Japanese, Thai, Vietnamese, Indian and the like.

My daydreams carry me away, to thoughts of my childhood. Before I left Singapore to study in Adelaide, I was surrounded by my large extended family, all of whom loved food and many of whom were very good cooks.

My mum was no cook, but she knew when a dish was cooked well. The cooks were Aunt Vivien, Aunt Mary and Uncle Ron. Aunt Vivien was a master chef and she cooked Nonya cuisine with distinction. Another big influence on my love of food and cooking was the principal of my school, Mrs Ellice Handy, who was one of the first Asian women to publish a recipe book featuring hawker food, Nonya food and Singaporean home cuisine.

Nonya cooking is a blend of Chinese and Malay cuisines. The descendants of the early Chinese in the Straits Settlement of Penang, Malacca and Singapore were known as 'Perankan'—meaning 'someone born locally'. The women of this group were called 'Nonya' and the men called 'baba'.

Why do we carry on about food to such an extent compared to other races? Well, it has to be noticed that the English discuss the weather at length and Australians talk about sport a lot.

In our family, I recall the frequent banquets that my dad held at home. A group of cooks and assistants would come to the house and set up a kitchen outside where they would cook the banquet. These banquets were given in honour of visiting senior officials from the Nissan Group or General Motors. The officials would attend the banquets with their wives, and they not only talked about cars, they also chatted about Chinese food, mainly Cantonese cuisine, with the sweet and sour pork or honey king prawns.

For a family treat, when Mum and Dad were in a good mood, we were allowed to stay up late and go for a short drive to a hawker spot for supper and have the best Hokkien Mee. This place was dimly lit by streetlights and was nothing more than a couple of stalls beside the gutter, with round wooden tables and stools. There was usually a soft breeze, the tropical smell of humid earth mixed with the aroma of frangipani flowers, and the delicate steam of sweet chicken broth wafting from the big pots at the stalls. We could have plain mee—a thick yellow wheat noodle, or bee hoon—a thinner rice noodle. I could never make up my mind and would dither until my mum would call out impatiently, "Come on Bernice, if you can't make up your mind, no mee for you, lah."

"I'll have bee hoon mee," I would reply—a mixture of both noodles. We would chat happily amongst ourselves until the bowls of steaming chicken broth arrived, topped with a sprinkle of green spring onion and white pepper. After we finished, a little girl would come over and put sweets on the table. My dad would take the sweets and give them to us. He would then give the little girl some coins. Mother would say, "Ah-yah, you always encourage them!" and Dad would reply, "It's alright, Phyl." Then we'd all hop back into the car, feeling sleepy, with full tummies.

During long games of Mahjong with her sisters and brothers, seated under a slowly turning ceiling fan to bring some relief from the tropical heat, Mum would compare notes with them on which restaurant had the best pork crackle.

"I had the best crackle yesterday. So good, lah! You put in your mouth, bite one time, softly, and go into half, then just melt in mouth. So good!" my mother would begin.

"Where you go?" Auntie Mary replied.

"Orchard Road of course, lah!"

Auntie Mary's eyebrows raised. "Bet you paid a lot. I know of restaurant in Chinatown that has crackle as good, maybe better, and half the price!"

"I don't believe!' my mother furrowed her brow to emphasise her incredulity. "Also, you know, I hear that Australian pork got strong smell. Our Singapore pork, no smell. They say that Australian pig eat wheat and ours eat fruit and vegetables, so ours more healthy, and no smell, lah."

Uncle Ron rolled his eyes, "Hey, you want to play Mahjong or talk about pigs. Your turn, lah!"

The sisters would collapse in giggles and swear in Malay at Uncle Ron.

On other occasions, we would be out with my uncles and aunties at the hawker stall. "You know, Bert, this char siew is just sooo good," Aunt Mary would sigh.

"Nothing like the shop in Killiney Road, lah," Uncle Ron jumped in.

"Ahyah, why you all bother, Vivien can do this 200 per cent better!" Uncle Robert said dismissively.

"Okay, okay, don't fight, this one is very good, lah!" Aunt Vivien laughed, breaking the rising tension.

Growing up with these experiences of chatting about food was wonderful, observing the fun, closeness and social bonding that it created, adding layer upon layer to the fond relationships we all shared.

After moving to Adelaide, my Asian friends and I missed our spicy food. I wanted to cook Asian food to connect socially with my friends, and to introduce my husband to the incredible array of flavours that I had grown up with. Unfortunately, during the sixties and seventies, there was only one Chinese café in Adelaide, on Hindley Street, and we had difficulty even getting soy sauce in the supermarkets. In frustration, John and I opened an Asian grocery store so we could get the basics like dark and light soya sauce, bean sprouts, chilli sauce, cinnamon, turmeric, cardamom, cloves, star anise and the like. But we were too busy with our medical careers and the shop did not last long.

Over the many years of observing family, close friends,

acquaintances and my father's business colleagues, I can only conclude that talking about food is not inane chatter, nor is it a flawed racial characteristic—it is a means of finding common ground, to put new friends at ease, to banter with close friends, and to strengthen the bonds with family.

***

Further memories of my immediate family are the way my father would combine his business with our family holidays, taking us 'up country' to visit his car spare parts agents.

These working holidays involved packing the family and the luggage into my father's Opel sedan and driving across the causeway that separated Singapore from what was then called Malaya, before travelling up the peninsula.

After crossing the border from Singapore into Malaya, we would have to wait for what seemed to be hours before we could cross over into the township of Johore Bahru, in of the State of Johore. While we waited to cross, my father would ask us to name the makes of the cars around us, by looking at their logos. If you didn't know, you were ridiculed. There was no *'how long now?'* We knew from previous experience that we would be punished if we complained, by having a reduced lunch or dinner, and have to sit on our own.

Once we could cross over, on we drove to our lunch spot at a place called Kajang. This was where the best satay was to be had, from the local hawker centre, a rectangular building square grey concrete columns holding up the roof. Inside were long concrete tables, accompanied by long continuous seating. The air was hot and humid, but we did not notice as we hurriedly chose our seats.

There were lots of people sitting around, surrounded by hawkers busily attending to their satay sticks, which they grilled over red-hot coals and arranged on plates with sliced cucumber, onions and rice patties wrapped in pandan leaves. The aroma of the cooking satay-marinated chicken and beef pierced onto wooden skewers was mouth-watering. Mixed with the thick pungent smell of the dipping sauce, it was just too delicious. We ordered, we gobbled and we washed it down with sugar cane water.

After Kajang, we would travel on to my dad's agent in Seremban. We called the family there 'Auntie' and 'Uncle'—it was the custom to do that that even though they were not actually family.

Seremban was a lot cooler than Singapore, and had a calm atmosphere. Each time we visited, my Auntie and Uncle would smile at my parents and fondly tell them, "Your children are so big, they are so good, they have changed so much, they look good, you are so lucky…"

When we left Serembang and wound our way up to Frasers Hill, we started our real holiday. The road up to Frasers Hill was very windy, and on the first trips there I was very carsick. But as we went there often, I became more comfortable.

The journey up Frasers Hill ended when we arrived at our bungalow—Singapore House. The temperature there was in the low twenties, instead of the thirties, and the humidity was at least fifty per cent lighter than Singapore. It was lovely and cool. The bungalow had dark wood floors and three or four bedrooms in each corner, with a central open area, which had an open fireplace, a sitting space and a dining area, where we delighted in the food that was produced by our Hakka cook—especially his roast beef with an Eastern garlic flavour.

We loved being at Singapore House, as we got to wear our woollens and skip around in the crisp air with no stickiness on our skin. We would walk for miles, marvelling at the wild orchids growing along the forest trails. We would search for the monkey cup—a plant in the shape of a cup, with liquid in it. We were told that monkeys drank from them, even though I don't think there were any monkeys there.

This is a beautiful memory of a bygone time.

***

I think about my large extended family, led by my grandfather, Chia Yee Soh and populated by his nineteen children—my aunts and uncles—and us, his numerous grandchildren, too many to recall.

I was born in 1938, just before World War II. The guns in Singapore pointed south, towards the sea, and the Japanese were coming down the Malaya Peninsula from the north.

We left Singapore for Australia before I turned two. The banks were closed, but Grandfather did not believe in banks and kept his money under his mattress, so he had the money to take eleven of us to Australia. The family members chosen to go were my grandfather, my two grandmothers, my mother, my Aunt Janet, three of my mother's teenaged brothers—Uncle Ron, Uncle Harold and Uncle Willie—and the three grandchildren—my elder brother Leslie, my cousin Kenny (Aunt Janet's son) and me.

Extended family. I am in front of window.

My dad and other uncles stayed in Singapore. We landed in Sydney in 1940 and returned to Singapore in 1945 after the war had ended. I was seven when we returned to Singapore, and I didn't know my father at all. I recall Aristotle's words, "Give me a child until he is seven, and I will show you the man." I never got to know my father well as he was always very busy building his car business.

In Sydney, my mother was very ambitious. She went to the University of Sydney to do an arts course and became a teacher. We were looked after by our two grandmothers while my mother studied. When I was four years old, I was sent to kindergarten at Ravenswood School, as we lived in Killara. I now live in Killara, about a two-minute drive away from where I lived during World War II, approximately seventy-five years ago. I was unhappy and lonely at kindergarten, and I must have made a fuss as I didn't attend for long. My brother Leslie went to the local public school.

When we returned to Singapore in 1945, my seven-year-old eyes saw a rundown, desolate place, with paper money strewn on the ground. I remembered that I was so excited and ran to gather the money only to be told that it was Japanese and not worth anything. My brother Laurence was born after the war. He is ten years my junior. I was close to him as, although he had a maid to look after him, he preferred to be with me. I used to carry him and feed him and felt very happy to be allowed to look after him. We are still very close. Although there is only one year's age difference between my brother Leslie and me, we had different interests and attended different schools, so we did not communicate much.

I was very happy at school. Apart from being conscientious in my academic work, I also loved sports of all kinds. I represented my school in athletics, swimming and netball, as well as in debating. I still retain the friendships I made then, and when I return to Singapore, we still got together for a Nonya meal.

When my brothers and I were growing up, our parents were very busy and we were looked after by our maid. This meant that we did not bond very strongly with our parents, especially with our father. I noticed that being a boy was an advantage as my brothers were considered for any benefits before I was. I would ask why I wasn't considered and was accused of being too determined and independent. Maybe I was—those traits have stood me in good stead during my life.

All of this meant that I considered myself happy at school but sad at home. Looking from the outside, it would have been easy to assume that I would have been very happy at home. After we returned from Australia we lived in a bungalow with a small garden. The house was raised on pillars, with space under the house for storage and for a dog kennel. The house was on one level, with windows all around. There were three bedrooms, with a small verandah leading off the two smaller bedrooms. My classmates lived in bungalows or terraced homes with a central open area open to the sky, or in units or shop houses. These shop houses were unique. They were terraced houses with a small shop on the ground floor and the living area on the first floor. They were usually located in busy and noisy commercial areas. At the time, these houses were looked upon as very basic. Today, they are sought-after iconic treasures.

After a few years we moved to a bigger house—a two-storey home with four bedrooms. In spite of the material wealth, I still wasn't happy as I was poor in emotional wealth. To me, the emotional wealth of love, affection and friendship is the wealth that is paramount, and which cannot be bought.

As my school was Methodist, religion featured strongly during my childhood. We used to sing hymns every Friday in the assembly hall, and this brought joy to all of us. We also had scripture and had missionaries visiting from America. They used to fascinate me, with their free and relaxed way of teaching. They encouraged questions, which was a novelty as we were used to adults taking the approach that children should be seen and not heard.

These days, as a medical practitioner, I query the religious beliefs that I was raised with, but the faith given in the first seven years of my life is still hard to forsake.

***

Knock, knock, knock.

"Can you open up, please. It's the health team here to take your COVID-19 swab."

I pulled myself back to the present and opened the door. A woman dressed in blue, her face obscured by a mask and visor, swabbed my nostril and throat. "Thank you," she said, and rushed away.

By then, the sun was shining in through the back window. Sunset. The colours of orange, ochre and burnt sienna swirled around the fast-sinking orb, and I was transported back to the wide-open spaces of Woomera.

***

I walk onto my comfortable balcony and gazed at the vastness of the landscape of Woomera, all the way to the horizon, revelling in the colours and the silky blackness that followed. The clean, crisp air and the bright, clearly defined stars are the perfect antidote to the days, which are filled with the heat of the desert and the desperate misery of the asylum seekers.

I look up at the distinct image of the Southern Cross, the Milky Way, and the brightness of Sirius, thinking of Oday and his fellow asylum seekers, just ten minutes' drive away at the detention centre.

Oday has been locked up for over two years now, and has fallen into a deep depression, without hope and without family.

"Never give up," I tell him, and he raises a weak smile that seems to be for my benefit, rather than through any belief in my words.

The contrast between the beautiful, open, free night sky and the razor wire of the detention centre is heartbreaking. Feeling the weight of it all, I walk back inside.

The Bob Dylan song 'Blowing in the Wind' rises up in my consciousness. His breathtaking lyrics evoke in me the question of whether I can look the other way and be oblivious to the cry for freedom?

I think of the strident call of a politician in his recent election speech, "We will decide who comes to this country and the circumstances in which they come."

Where is the care? Where is the compassion?

***

During the time I was at Woomera my emotions had to be controlled in order to effectively fulfill my role as a medical practitioner.

I will now undo the tether on my unhappy emotions and share with you what it was like. On a daily basis, signs of depression were everywhere—the hunched postures and sad expressions of the adults were ubiquitous, while the children were abnormally quiet. When frustrations tipped over into anger and a refugee would fight with a security officer, he would be placed in isolation. An isolated man put into further isolation. I was furious, but I was powerless to affect change.

On a regular basis, refugees would sew up their lips, in protest at not having a voice. They would use a nail pulled from a piece of wood as the needle, and rough string as the thread. Can one imagine the pain? Can one imagine the desperation that pushes a person to do this? I set myself on automatic to do all that was required while I worked at Woomera, but my tears flowed silently down and my head felt like it might burst.

***

I am brought back to the present by another knock on the door. Even after just a few days in quarantine, I am used to the rhythm of the days, and I know that this time, the knock is to announce my evening meal. I open the door to retrieve the tray. As I sit at the small table and begin to eat, my thoughts turn back to John Howard's words. I wonder if I would have felt as welcome in Australia if a similar speech had been made just before my arrival, back in 1958.

With John Howard, former Prime Minister of Australia.

CHAPTER 3

University Days

When I was growing up in Singapore in the 1950s, girls were thought to be less intellectually able than boys. This perception of inadequacy meant that I frequently wished I was a boy. This desire was cemented when I declared that I wanted to go to university. My older brother, Leslie, was already overseas, studying engineering in Adelaide, South Australia. On his visits home, he would tempt me with tales of excitement and daring, and so I also wanted to go to Adelaide, to study medicine.

My mother was having none of it.

"You should be happy to marry a Singaporean millionaire. Your father and I have already selected some suitable bachelors," she declared.

I was horrified! Marry someone I did not know? I persisted, but she still could not understand my desire.

"Why do you want to be a doctor? Being a nurse would be enough."

I totally disagreed and we argued at length.

"I don't care what you say! You let Leslie go to Adelaide, so why can't I? It's because I'm a girl, isn't it? I hate you all! I'm going to Adelaide, I'm going to study medicine, and I'm going to marry whomever I like! So there!"

My mother's face looked grim and furious. I was quaking inside. In Asian culture you are not to answer back to your parents. It is a sign of disrespect and bad upbringing.

"I don't care," I said again, then ran into the bathroom and looked at myself in the mirror above the washbasin. My face was contorted with fury, fear and frustration. I cried and cried and cried.

After this, there was a lengthy stand-off of silence. I moped around, making myself invisible in the dark corners of the house. One day, out of the blue, my dad finally broke the silence.

"Now, what do you want?"

I sweetly and politely told him that I just wanted to study medicine, and if not in Adelaide, then Singapore would do! Surprisingly, I was permitted to study in Australia, and in 1958 I began my studies.

***

It was deemed safer for me to stay at a women's only college, as it was envisaged that there would be better control of our activities. My parents were nervous about the promiscuous culture that was rumoured of young Westerners.

However, the only women's college was St Ann's, and there were no vacancies. As a short-term solution, I looked for private lodgings. At one house, a kind elderly lady told me, "Dear, I would really love to have you, but I'm too old to be washing sheets every day, when your brown colour soils my bed linen." My jaw dropped in disbelief. In the end, I found a room in a cottage in the suburb of St Peters, sharing with another female student.

Before too long, I secured accommodation at St Ann's, and what a difference it was! From a quiet, small cottage with an elderly landlady and one roommate, I was suddenly in a large college, with forty to fifty residents. The college was walking distance from the medical school, along Frome Road, winding past wide grassy parklands, filled with bursts of pale pastels and bright pinks, yellows and reds from the abundance of roses, their delicate perfume lingering in the morning dew. I would breathe in the scent as I walked with my fellow medical students, deep in discussion about the names of the muscles, veins, arteries and nerves that we'd had to memorise for our latest anatomy viva.

The walk continued past the Children's Hospital on the right and the zoo on the left, with its sounds of the roars and chattering and shrieks of various animals. On approaching the medical school the rows of parallel plane trees on either side of Frome Road arched over to form a tunnel of green. So beautiful and cool: a welcome barrier against the unforgiving Australian sun. Some distance away, across the parklands, stood the majestic St Peter's Cathedral, with its towering steeple.

Coming from Singapore, where parks were infrequent and the crowds of people hurrying and pushing along intermingled with the fumes of diesel and traffic jams, Adelaide was enchanting and tranquil, with its wide-open spaces, quaint bluestone cottages and rush reed fences, humming with bees and fragrant flowers, rather than discontent and diesel. A special place.

never handled a testis before, I approached the task with caution. I lightly touched and tapped the reddish-blue organ. The surgical consultant bellowed, "Dr Eu, you aren't playing the piano!"

I felt a flush cover my neck and face, and meekly replied, "Sir, I haven't examined one of these before."

The class collapsed in laughter, to which the consultant replied, "Doctors, she has a point here." I looked at his face. It was straight.

Another time, on a gynaecological ward round, a medical student in our group was asked to examine a cervix with a speculum—a metal device that helps to widen the vaginal passage so that one can see the end the cervix. As he was struggling to get a clear view, the speculum was slipping, and the patient was withdrawing. In a clear and desperate voice he implored, "Open wider please." Perhaps he would have been better off studying dentistry!

I've always liked to incise and stitch, and initially thought I might like to be a surgeon. I recall my first experience in an operating theatre, which was filled with the pungent odour of antiseptic. Tolerance to the smell builds up over time, but on that first day it was overwhelming. I stood, gazing round the theatre, when I felt a sharp tap on my shoulder—the head nurse, with hawk-eyes glinting behind her glasses smiled tightly.

"You must be the new medical student. Come along, we haven't got the whole day. Scrub up here, and make it thorough."

I scrubbed until I felt as though my skin was about to peel off. Once gowned and gloved, I tiptoed to the centre of the operating theatre, and in so doing brushed against an instrument cupboard. Hawk-eye was upon me once again.

"You touched that cupboard. You will have to regown."

Having regowned, and all set to assist, I approached the operating table, on which lay the patient, anaesthetised and ready. The table was at the level of my shoulder, and a voice boomed out, "She needs a stool!"

The voice came from Sir Surgeon, and the stool arrived immediately. I took position on the stool, opposite Sir Surgeon, and was ready. The operation was an appendicectomy. Drops of blood appeared at the initial incision.

"Wipe and retract!" boomed the voice.

I wiped, and used the retractor to widen the incision, revealing the yellow, lumpy subcutaneous fat beneath. A deeper incision, into the muscle, and blood oozed freely.

I dabbed, the blood still oozed. Sir Surgeon used a diathermy, sending an electric current to burn the ends of blood vessels and stem the bleeding. We incised along the direction of the muscle fibre, through the peritoneal membrane and into the abdominal cavity. He rummaged in the cavity and produced the infected appendix. Once the appendix was removed, the abdominal cavity was closed in layers: peritoneal membrane, muscle, fat, and skin. Suture and cut, suture, and cut. When I disrobed and removed my gloves, I found I was drenched through with sweat.

Although working in the operating theatre was stressful, it was a great experience and did not deter me from taking up surgery as a specialist option.

A medical course is full-on, with lectures on the hour, every hour, five days a week, with a lunch break of an hour. I knew that some of my colleagues did not attend the lectures, but it was not in my culture nor in my psyche to miss a lecture, unless I was ill. As Asian students, our thoughts were that our parents paid and sent us all the way to Adelaide, and we could not think of failing them by not doing our best. Indeed, we often struggled when we had to cut out attending enticing social functions. Especially when we had not completed an assignment and deadlines were looming or end of term examinations were approaching. We could not bring ourselves not to comply with the dictates of our course.

While in St Ann's College, we missed our Asian food badly as the college food was entirely Western. So, at weekends, a group of us girls from Asian countries—mainly from Singapore, Malaysia, and Hong Kong—would go shopping for meat, vegetables, rice and spicy condiments. The college had a kitchen in the basement of one of the buildings, where we could cook. There were some excellent cooks, too. They would produce curries, spicy tofu, noodles, sweet and sour pork, rendang and a variety of vegetable concoctions. We would then ask our room-mates and other girls from the college to join us. I believe they enjoyed these cook ups. Although some more than others.

***

There were three of us, Helen Handy, Lau Boung Gee and myself, from Singapore who studied medicine together in Adelaide. We met in Primary 1 at the Methodist Girls' School and went all the way through school together until we sat for our Higher School Certificate. This HSC was taken in Singapore and marked in Cambridge, England. The certificate was not available in our girls' school—I presume that girls were not expected to achieve this level of education. So we went to our brother school, the Anglo Chinese School, to obtain the HSC, with which we had to have achieved straight As in all six subjects if we wanted to be accepted into the University of Adelaide.

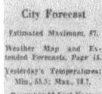

The Advertiser

WITH WHICH IS INCORPORATED "THE REGISTER"

Adelaide, South Australia, Saturday, December 15, 1962.

OVER MILLION SALES WEEKLY
Audited Net Sales Exceed 193,000 Daily

AINST REBEL REMNANTS
RILLA FIGHT
R IN
NEO

THEIR BIG DAY

BRITAIN'S IN EUROPE REV

PLEA TO OTHER NATIONS

CANBERRA, Dec. 14.—The Minister for External Affairs (Sir Garfield Barwick) tonight appealed for non-interference from outside in the Brunei uprising.

Venus Shot Fails To Respond

NEW YORK, December 14.
The spacecraft Mariner II today failed to respond to two attempts to start a scanning device designed to pierce the perpetual cloud surrounding the planet Venus.

Plane's Fog Landing Fails: Three Die

BRISBANE, December 14.
Three men were fatally injured at Toowoomba tonight when their aircraft smashed into a power pole while attempting a roadside landing in thick fog.

THIEF GRABS PAYROLL IN CITY OFFICE

Your Saturday Magazine

We ploughed through six years of medicine and graduated in 1963, it seemed to flash by, leaving us with bittersweet memories. The three of us, together with another seven primary schoolmates, are still friends and keep in contact to this day. We are now in our eighties and are known as the Evergreens.

Although they were demanding and laborious times, I felt that medicine was a vocation, and I'd fought to be allowed to do it, so the stress of the studies was well worth it.

Even so, many years later, I wondered if my medical training would be sufficient to cope with the unusual tasks that would be demanded of me at the Woomera Detention Centre.

CHAPTER 4
Woomera Detention Centre

It seemed that I'd hit the ground running. As the only doctor, I had no opportunity to gently ease into the role. From the moment I started, I was busy treating acute diseases including tonsillitis, renal infection and pneumonia, along with traumatic lacerations and fractures.

About a month before I started at Woomera Detention Centre, I had worked for a private health organisation in Adelaide that sent doctors out to the Woomera township once a week, to carry out physical checks on the newly arrived asylum seekers. They were bussed from the detention centre in groups of ten. It was during one of these weekly locum trips to the township that a riot broke out at the centre, and my assessment clinic was consequently cancelled.

The asylum seekers had pushed down the chain-link fence and walked out. They proceeded—men, women, and children—to march peacefully to the township, which had a population of 700.

Late that afternoon, I went out to observe the scene. The sun was setting. The huge golden globe was sinking, sending streaks of vivid jewel colours into the intense sapphire sky. A splendid sight. In the near distance, emus and kangaroos grazed contentedly.

My attention turned to the group from the detention centre—a ragged lot of men and women, slim teenagers and young children. They were gathered at the edge of the township. Most of them sat on the pavement or on the sandy, dusty ground. Mothers were hugging their children, trying to keep them warm within the folds of their voluminous garments. It was beginning to get cool, and I was dressed in only my t-shirt and jeans. I shivered, not only from the cold, but from the sight of the asylum seekers.

Soon it would be bitterly cold. I noticed some of the townspeople giving the mothers blankets and others handing out water. The guards from the centre strode around, looking angry, frustrated, belligerent and authoritative, with their batons pushing and shoving the asylum seekers together. After a while, the guards seemed to get them under control, at which time I was called away.

As I sat on my balcony some weeks later, feeling the vastness of the landscape silently exuding a stillness and freedom, I thought back to that afternoon. It seemed impossible that just a stone's throw away, I had witnessed the turmoil and upheaval and lack of freedom of people—many of whom were refugees, not criminals.

After the riot, I'd heard that the asylum seekers were finally rounded up and returned to the centre, but that there were around seven male asylum seekers still at large. I'd wondered how these seven must be, in the harsh, cold, empty bush lands that stretched out around the detention centre. After about a week they were all recaptured, and I am sure it must have been a relief.

I do believe that this incident was a direct result of the long wait without any information about their loved ones back home or of the progress of their visa applications. Even people convicted of crimes know when they will be released.

After the fence escapade, a double metal chain-linked fence was erected, with double razor wire on top, surrounding the whole of the detention centre. It was a forbidding sight.

It was only a few weeks after this that I was asked whether I would like to work inside the detention centre. By that time, I had assessed about fifty detainees, and all, without exception, appeared very grateful. I accepted the offer, as I thought I could contribute to easing their undoubted stresses.

***

When I started at the Woomera Detention Centre, I found that a typical day could be broken up into two types of work. My priority, and the majority of my work, was clinical medical. However, I felt that I must find out how the asylum seekers lived in this environment. I had a sense that this sort of observation would help me to understand their illnesses better. The health staff disagreed and suggested that it is a waste time.

But whenever I had ten or fifteen minutes to spare, I would slip off to observe life behind the wire.

I saw that there was always a queue at breakfast, lining up for toast. There were four or five toasters, each toasting five pieces of bread at a time, for 1,000 stressed people.

I noted there was a pecking order among the Middle Eastern people. The order was first Iranians, then Iraqis, then Afghanis. However, when it came to the toast, this pecking order was disregarded. It was first come, first served, including children. One morning, as I watched, one of the toasters broke down. My expectation of what would happen next quickly played out. The offending toaster was smashed, and the previously orderly queue descended into chaos. It could be said that they should have known to behave better. But with highly stressed individuals and a loss of self-esteem, it does not take much to cause pandemonium.

In another instance, I asked an asylum seeker what he did when he rose each morning. He blithely replied, "We go to muster in the morning and then again at night."

What would some of these self-respecting people who have come from dignified and distinguished lineage think, if they were aware of the connotation of that Australian slang? I wondered.

Indeed, Oday did finally summon the courage to ask me why I didn't like the word "muster". I had to explain that we usually use the word muster when we herd animals together to count them, to make sure we haven't lost any.

He wasn't happy.

In spite of these inappropriate expressions, the asylum seekers spoke well of being given somewhere to live. It was only when there was a perceived lack of respect towards them that tensions rose.

An experience highlighted this for me.

A nurse asked me to visit an asylum seeker, as he had not come out of his donga, nor had he had anything to eat for some days. As I had never been in the donga area, it was a good opportunity to check the place out.

It is a very hot day, in the mid-thirties, with the harsh Australian sun shining mercilessly through the clear blue sky. The ultraviolet rays seared my face, arms and neck as I walked and walked between the rows of dongas, with the hot, dry wind blowing the red dust up into my eyes. I passed by several opened doors, where miserable faces nodded in greeting and murmured, 'visa' to me. A totally unhappy and downcast group of people. The children were subdued.

After we had passed hundreds of dongas, I was directed to stop.

I asked permission to enter. I could see that there was a bunk bed against the wall, and a mat on the floor at the entrance. The patient was lying on the mat, with only six inches of bare space between him and the entranceway. If you were in a hurry to enter, you would have to step on part of the mat, which was made of woven rushes of bright red and green.

I thought, *He is watching whether I respect him. I have to avoid stepping on his mat.* It is the Asian custom to show respect with facial expressions or body language, and so I delicately tiptoed past him, trying to step only on the bare floor, and not on the mat.

I succeeded.

When I looked back at him, he nodded and glanced at the mat.

I was then able to get him to agree to step out of the donga, and to eat and drink.

Usually though, rather than going out to the dongas to treat my patients, they came into the clinic—with a wide variety of needs. A typical day looked like this:

First thing in the morning, a pregnant Iranian woman came in for a check-up. Her baby had previously been deemed to be an 'unstable lie', which meant that her baby had moved from the normal position of headfirst in the pelvis, to presenting bottom-first—called the 'breech' position. On examination, her baby was now presenting normally again, headfirst. Having worked in the Kandang Kerbau maternity hospital in Singapore, I was fully alert to the risk that can occur with an unstable lie. Even though the baby was presenting normally, I wasn't going to take any chances, as the nearest hospital was in Port Augusta, nearly 200 kilometres and a two-hour drive from the Woomera Detention Centre. In order to ensure the mother and baby were safe, I alerted the obstetrician at the hospital that we

As these men refused to drink, the next step was to mandatorily rehydrate them through intravenous drip. To do this, one had to phone the federal parliamentary secretary. I phoned the relevant person and left a message for permission to mandatorily rehydrate them.

It took ages to get a reply.

Meanwhile, I was left with the high risk of collapse in any one of the men in the group. After six or seven hours, consent was given. The men were escorted by guard to the Woomera Hospital.

Dr Lockwood did the necessary intravenous rehydration, but he was not amused.

There was also an attempted hanging later that day, but I did not treat the person. I asked Oday whether the man was alright, and he replied that he was OK. I was not informed as to his condition, nor did I follow up with him. If this incident had taken place in the early weeks of my arrival at the centre, it would have caused me great concern not to have examined the man to ensure he was okay. Now, I took Oday at his word. I wondered if I was getting desensitised.

It would not have been surprising. In between the pregnant woman, the insomniacs, the man who had eaten the gravel, and the children who needed immunisations, I had treated injuries including physical lacerations sustained in riots, infections of lips that had been sewn together, infections of the skin and lungs, and infectious diseases.

And so it was, while treating these acute medical issues, that I became aware that there was always the hidden spectre of mental health disorder lurking just beneath the surface: especially PTSD (post-traumatic stress disorder), which was endemic in the population of the detention centre.

I contacted several psychiatrists in Adelaide, but due to the controversial issue of the asylum seekers, they all declined to assist with treating the people at the detention centre. I was totally disgusted that they were thinking of their careers rather than helping people in need!

In the end, I got in touch with a prominent psychiatrist from Melbourne, Dr Harry Minas. To my relief, he agreed to come. He was very helpful, and also communicated his concerns to the Minister for Immigration, Philip Ruddock. In an article on asylum seekers, Dr Minas said, "As the global challenge of displacement continues to grow and become more complex, we will have to do considerably better than we are doing now."[1]

In the detention centre, aside from the numerous physical illnesses that afflicted the adults, I was concerned with the development of the children in such a chaotic environment. To this end, I urged my psychologist friend, Dr Marie O'Neill, an experienced child psychologist specialising in child abuse, to be part of our health team caring for the 200 children in detention.

Keeping children in the centre for such a long period of time can be looked upon as child abuse. Marie, after some urging, came and joined the team. She ended up staying at the centre longer than I did, and she did her best. I believe she gave evidence in an inquiry concerning children in the Woomera Detention Centre. She commented that she was concerned but said, "I think I was protected against finding too much."

Due to rumours that there was child abuse, the health team was

---

[1] From a public lecture at the Canstan Centre for Human Rights Law, Monash University, 13 February 2013.

always vigilant. Dr Simon Lockwood at Woomera Hospital and I did not observe any such abuse, nor were any children referred to us citing abuse.

With all these concerns, Simon and I decided to write a document, itemising the concerns that we encountered. We then met with Minster Ruddock to explain the document and its proposed recommendations. He said that he would read it and consider it.

Some of the recommendations were implemented, such as an increase in mental health professionals in the centre, and the integration of the asylum seeker children into the local schools in the township. The original immigration department manager, Mr Tony Hamilton-Smith, was a key supporter of integrating the detainees into the local community.

But acute incidents continued to occur, and immediate responses were needed. The day I have described here is a typical day.

But if it had been a Tuesday, it might have been a different story!

CHAPTER 5

War Zone in South Australia

It is Tuesday.

Oday is still in limbo. He brings an Iraqi man into the clinic, enjoining me, "See him, Doctor. He just give up!"

A guard follows closely behind them, desperately trying to re-establish his authority with the words, "I'll take him in!" Oday ignores the guard, and marches into the clinic.

The man has a deep gash on his forearm, which is bleeding profusely. I apply pressure to stop the bleeding. He struggles to be released, voicing his strong objections in Arabic, in a tone that lets me know he doesn't want to be treated.

Oday barks an order to him in Arabic and the man calms down. It is Tuesday, so I am not surprised. I expect more of such incidents today.

But right now, this man, whose name I will quickly forget, needs my attention.

Oday makes him lie down on the examination couch. His self-inflicted wound needs a dozen stitches. I stretch his arm on a splint, explaining through Oday that I am going to give him local anaesthetic and put in a few stitches to close up his laceration. I prepare the anaesthetic, but before I can administer it, he pulls his arm away. He says something in Arabic and, much to my incredulity, Oday tells me that he doesn't need an injection, and that I can just sew the cut.

"Tell him that the injection will stop the pain!" I exclaim.

Oday translates, and the patient says something in Arabic that ends with *Inshallah!*

I shrug and abandon the anaesthetic. I start to put in the stitches. The man doesn't even flinch. I am sweating profusely. In order to work as quickly as possible, I put in continuous running stitches instead of individual stitches, feeling the sensitive skin under my needle. He still gives no sign that he is experiencing any pain. The pain appears to have been transmitted to me.

After a while, I have finished. The patient sits up, takes the tail end of the nylon thread and with one mighty pull, rips the whole lot out, then, with a tight grunt, he jumps off the couch and walks out.

"Sorry, Doc. He no manners," Oday apologises, before disappearing after the man.

Every Tuesday, a list is published, with the names of the people who have been granted a Temporary Protection Visa, freeing them from detention. Those *not* named can either go back from whence they came, or continue to wait in detention indefinitely.

In limbo.

So, every Tuesday the asylum seekers line up along the fence in the hope that a Temporary Protection Visa will be granted to them. The expressions on most of their faces show signs of anxiety, doubt and sadness. The faces on the group that have recently arrived still shine with hope. When names are called out, there are cries of immense relief and joy—from those who have been included on the list. But for those whose names are not called, which is the majority, watching their response is unbearable. There is nobody to counsel the leftovers.

Some in the group will quietly walk away, some will utter curses, and a few will let out cries of dismay. Their chaotic responses infect everyone who has been disappointed, and a riot is born. As Martin Luther King Jr said, a riot is the language of the unheard.

As a result, every Tuesday was riot day. People with lacerations to their limbs and bodies would come to the medical centre. There were times when the lights would go out and I would have to continue stitching by candle light, my hands shaking with anger that these episodes were allowed to occur week after week, my eyesight straining to see in the candlelight, sweat pouring from me in the closeness of the small room, which was packed with people trying to escape the brutality of the guards, as well as those needing medical attention.

The first Tuesday after I begin working at the detention centre, I look out of a small window of my tiny clinic, helplessly watching the scene unfold. I can feel the heat of their devastation with as much intensity as I can hear their cries of humanity. What start as waves of compassion quickly turns into anger and outrage, flooding my whole being.

This will happen every Tuesday.

I march straight to see the manager. He tells me it's the fault of the system.

Meanwhile, unrest is simmering in the Woomera Detention Centre. It starts with a loud rhythmic alarm and the closing of all gates, including the main exit gate.

I am also shut in. There is the sudden roar as water cannons batter the desperate people and stern orders are barked out, lost amongst the screams of fright, anguish and pain.

Smoke from fires that have been lit across the compound fills my eyes and nostrils, and there is the brittle sound of breaking windows, accompanied by more screams of pain. All these sounds and activities swirl around the medical centre. I cannot see what is happening beyond the thin walls of the hut. The nurses go out to help, while I remain in the clinic to receive the wounded. It is difficult to concentrate on attending and treating the injured, who begin to stream in. I presume the medical centre is guarded, as no asylum seekers come in to attack us. In fact, many asylum seekers come to the medical centre simply to seek refuge.

Patients pour in, with swellings and lacerations covering their limbs and faces. Suddenly, the clinic door bangs open, and a muscular guard supporting another guard with a pronounced limp burst into the room. He has a fractured ankle.

I give him an injection of morphine and proceed to stabilise the ankle. I ask if he is comfortable.

"Yes, thanks, Doc. I'm comfortable. Which is more than I can say for the guy who did this to me. I know who he is, and he's gonna regret it," he replies bitterly.

Before I can open my mouth to tell him that retaliation is not the right way to go, another guard ushers me away to my next three patients, all of whom have large lacerations, requiring stitches.

As all the registered nurses are outside, tending to the wounded and sending the more severely injured patients to the clinic, I have to request that my psychologist friend, Marie, help me cut the nylon thread as I suture the wounds. Then all the lights go out in the clinic. I call for candles, which come readily. I continue suturing, with the help of Marie. She is eager, but has the shakes.

Sometimes she cuts too close to the knot, and completely unravels the stitch. Other times she cuts too wide, leaving a long thread tailing out of the suture. After a while, she overcomes her nervousness and cuts perfectly. Taking into account that she has never done such a job before, she is excellent.

Later, another two Afghanis are sent to the clinic, with their lips sewn together. I quickly cut the stitches, apply antiseptic to their wounds, and give them oral antibiotics.

It feels more like a war zone than rural South Australia.

Thankfully, over time, the riots become less frequent—but that afternoon, I have to ask myself, if I've made the right decision in taking the position.

***

I worked at Woomera Detention Centre from December 1999 to September 2000—just nine months of a year's contract. I could not continue.

Dr Simon Lockwood from Woomera Hospital continued part-time, visiting the detention centre in the mornings on a daily basis.

The centre was finally closed in 2003.

CHAPTER 6

Medical Internship & Further Medical Skills

If I had been told, back when I was a newly qualified doctor that I would have been not only witnessing the horrors of Woomera Detention Centre, but that I would be responsible for caring for the medical needs of thousands of desperate asylum seekers, I would have found it hard to imagine.

After I qualified, I undertook a one-year internship at the Royal Adelaide Hospital, where my time was to be divided into four sessions each of three months' duration. I was a fresh-faced Miss Know-it-all, ready for my initial sessions at the Casualty Department, now known as Accident and Emergency. Little did I know that the skills I acquired during those months would provide the foundation for the much-needed skills required at Woomera.

The cases seen in casualty were mainly related to vehicular accidents. I saw severe bone fractures, trauma of internal organs leading to possible internal bleeding, and more.

One accident that has always stayed with me was a motorcycle accident involving a twenty-year old. As I entered the casualty cubicle, I saw that the patient had half his face covered with a sterile gauze dressing. I casually removed the dressing and spontaneously dropped the gauze on the floor. The left side of his face was pushed in, swollen and bruised and a round object was dangling on a membrane from his lower eyelid, resting on his cheekbone below. His left eyelid was puffy and closed. With sterile forceps, I slowly and gently lifted the membrane, expecting to see a small stone. He jerked and shouted in extreme pain. I leapt backwards. The expected stone was his eye! As a new intern, it was unforgettable.

Our kids were never allowed to ride motorcycles—not even riding pillion. However, my son, who is now in his 50s, has a Harley Davidson, which is his pride and joy!

My second three-month session at the Royal Adelaide Hospital was in Ophthalmology (eyes). This session was uneventful, and involved treating infections and occasionally help with eye trauma. I had hoped to get involved in the excision of an eye for an eye transplant, but never had that opportunity.

I had another six months to complete at the Royal Adelaide Hospital, but it was not to be. Somehow, my parents had heard the whiff of a rumour that I was involved with a white Australian student—a final year medical student named John. He had large, round velvety eyes that shone kindness with every glance. He loved to joke the Aussie way, which to me is an exaggeration of situations. He was very 'ocker'.

To my surprise and delight, John loved Asian food. The first time I cooked for him, I chose a Malaysian curry, which is not too spicy.

"I hope this curry isn't too hot. It's not as hot as the Indian vindaloo curry," I said, as I served him a generous portion.

"I love curry," he assured me, and took a big mouthful before spluttering, "Bloody hell, where's the water jug?"

I rushed to pour him a glass, spilling half the water from the jug in the process.

He tipped the glass to his lips and glugged down a huge mouthful of water.

"Oh, sorry, sorry..." I said, devastated.

He had his back to me and coughed violently. I was almost in tears, wondering why I'd been so silly as to cook a curry. Then he turned around, grinning from ear to ear and said, "Oh, it's not too bad after all!"

I did not see the joke.

John was a very down to earth person, rocking up to see me in his crumpled shirt and pants. He took me to very modest cafés, where I was treated to pasties and fish and chips. My Asian girlfriends in Adelaide were not impressed. My parents and family back in Singapore would have been astounded, equating the standard of the places he took me with how much he valued me. I never told them the details of those outings.

And so it was with sadness that I had to leave Adelaide for Singapore, but family called and must be obeyed. So off I went, pulled back to Singapore, my parents hoping to put an end to this romance with a white man. John wondered why I didn't defy them. Although I was slowly absorbing the mores of Western culture, and becoming assertive and outspoken, at that stage I did not have the nerve to defy my parents.

Somewhere in the Bible, it says that when you have the child for seven years, you have them for the rest of their life. So it was without much resistance that I packed my bags and cancelled the remaining six-month session at the Royal Adelaide Hospital. I can't understand why I meekly obeyed, except that the biblical saying must have some truth. So John and I said our goodbyes, and promised to reunite in six months.

Back in my home country, I worked at the obstetrics and gynaecological hospital, Kandang Kerbau[2], meaning 'buffalo shed', referring to the area's history of buffalo rearing. In 1966, this well-known hospital was entered into the Guinness World Records for delivering the highest number of newborns within a single maternity facility. I was there at that time, when there were 100 deliveries per day. In Adelaide, it took a month to get our required quota of twenty deliveries. I was alone, as a green, newly trained doctor. My fellow interns, who had undertaken their studies in Singapore, were accustomed to such numbers, but I was overwhelmed. I, the Adelaide-trained doctor, had to take my time, and was meticulous and unhurried in my deliberations.

My work at the KK Hospital consumed me. I hardly saw my family. One time, my dad called me to say that he and mum were in the car park and wanted to see me as they had not seen me for days. When I met them in the hospital car park, my dad said, "Oh you smell of antiseptic!" I had not noticed. He then handed me a bag, saying, "Here are some char siew pow (barbeque pork buns), for you and the other doctors".

I thanked him, but thought to myself, *When will we have time to eat them?*

My dad wanted to see the doctors' lounge room. I couldn't understand why, and tried to brush him off by telling him I had to go back to work, but he wasn't having any of it, so I obediently trotted up to the nondescript lounge with my parents in tow. My dad gazed around the lounge, with its lumpy chairs and messy tables covered in hastily half-eaten plates food and abandoned and unfinished cans of drink. He looked unimpressed.

---

[2] Now known as the KK Women's and Children's Hospital.

"No TV for you hard-working doctors?" he exclaimed.

A few days later, a new TV arrived for the doctors' room. A gift from my dad. I was embarrassed, and also proud that he was so kind and caring. My father.

Back on the wards of KK Hospital there were pregnant women in active labour in individual cubicles. There were about twenty cubicles for the women with complications. These cubicles were full, all the time. Complications included high blood pressure, urinary tract infections, fever, breech presentation, abnormal proteins in the urine, and signs of foetal distress, all of which we had to monitor to help the mothers towards safe deliveries.

The other women in active labour—those without complications—had their babies delivered by midwives. There was another group of women who had delivered, but needed vaginal surgical repair. These post-partum (after the delivery) women were lined up on trollies along the hospital corridors, waiting for a doctor to become available to do the repairs. I cannot tell you how many trollies there were, but the trollies ran the whole length of the thirty-metre corridor.

I was totally swamped. I had never seen such high numbers of patients. We were run off our feet, watching over the women with complications, making decisions about when to refer them to consultants for caesarean sections, and when to proceed with a normal delivery.

With the vaginal surgical repairs, some were simple, while others were complex. The complex cases happened when there were no midwives or doctors available to assist at the delivery, resulting in bad tears. With so many repairs to perform, one learnt to do them rapidly, but meticulously and skilfully.

This part of my training helped me immensely with the numerous cuts and lacerations that I saw while I was at the Woomera Detention Centre.

Although this six-month obstetrics session was arduous and stressful, it was very satisfying. Kandang Kerbau Hospital helped me to cope with the few pregnant women at the Woomera Detention Centre, as we were required to assess when to keep the pregnant women until normal delivery and when to send them to the Port Augusta Hospital, a two-hour drive away.

I gained more experience with the complexities faced by individual patients when I did my general practice in Port Adelaide, as a locum to Dr Bob Elix. One day, an urgent call was allocated to me to visit a very sick woman in Semaphore who was having difficulty breathing. I hurried to her place, which was on the third floor of an apartment block, accessible only by the stairs. With my rather heavy doctor's bag, I skipped up to that floor, where I found a woman in her fifties, very short of breath. On listening to her lungs, I diagnosed an infection. I explained the problem to her and wrote a script for an antibiotic.

"I can't afford that, doctor. I'll be alright," she said.

"No, you will not," I replied, and then went and bought the antibiotic and delivered it to her, with the necessary follow up. Thank goodness for the introduction of Medicare.

More medical skills were added to my growing toolbox when I enrolled in a diploma course in child development in London. I later researched a screening tool to identify children who were delayed in their early development, between birth and the age of five years. This tool was known as the 'Woodside System for Screening General Development of the child' and was used in some parts of the

United Kingdom. The screening tool checked the development in the areas of gross motor skills, such as sitting, crawling and walking; fine motor skills, such as eye-hand coordination, grasping, holding and writing; auditory skills, such as babbling, single words, phrases and sentences; emotional responses to interaction at different stages, and monitoring vision and hearing.

I did a thesis on the Woodside development tool, which contributed to attaining a post-graduate Medical Doctorate (MD) from the University of Adelaide. I adapted this screening tool for South Australia, and introduced it for use by the nurses at the well-baby clinic in Adelaide.

I continued to diversify my skills by working in the treatment of people with drug addictions, in clinics in Adelaide and Sydney. This skill of treating drug addiction was much-needed in the Woomera Detention Centre. The main thrust of those drug addiction clinics is to try to eliminate or ameliorate the addiction of the patient to heroin or other substances. A complication of addiction is the toxic effect of contracting hepatitis B, hepatitis C, or HIV/AIDS, mainly through contaminated needles. The majority of the patients I met in these clinics also suffered from mental health issues. We had to not only treat our patients for their addictions, but also to counsel them for their mental health issues, with the help of psychologists and psychiatrists.

After gaining all of this experience, I thought that I was well qualified to work as a Special General Practitioner at the Woomera Detention Centre. Little did I know the extent of the turmoil bubbling beneath the surface, or the enormity of the mental health issues that existed, resulting in extreme levels of constant mayhem in the detention centre.

CHAPTER 7

Singapore & Family

I have always had a love of children and an interest in their development. So, when not seeing adult patients in the detention centre clinic, I like to wander over to the makeshift school. The teachers are wonderful in the way they are so dedicated and patient with the children. We know that the Woomera Detention Centre environment is in constant friction with the authorities, and incidents flaring up into riots is certainly not conducive to good child rearing, but the dedicated teachers and Marie, the child psychologist, made a difference.

Now that processing asylum seekers is being done offshore, in some unknown environment, the mental health of these children is of some concern. In the Woomera Detention Centre, I know that the parents showed high levels of stress, which would inevitably have an adverse impact on their children. This would be the case to an even greater degree if experienced staff were not available to assist the children.

My heart goes out to the children in Woomera Detention Centre, dragged away from their homelands, from the familiar sights, sounds, and smells, from their extended families of aunts, uncles, grandmothers, and grandfathers, to land in an isolated and unfriendly place. These children must have had a rich environment back in their homelands, as I did growing up in Singapore. The Australian detention centre must have felt like an extremely alien land.

I remember how excited I was when I returned to Singapore after a year studying in Adelaide. To see my family, my friends and my homeland again created emotions that were difficult to contain.

As I made my way down the steep metal steps of the plane, onto the hot tarmac of Singapore Airport, there was an oven-like whoosh of warm air on my face, carrying with it the smell of cinnamon, star anise, cumin, coriander, of flowers—hibiscus, frangipani, nonya malam—lady of the night, that was matched by the warmth of family greetings, enveloping me in a cosy and soft cocoon. I belonged. I was home.

The monsoon season has a special resonance with me. A heavy downpour falls, like a barrel of water has been poured right over your head. Then several blinding cracks of lightning and a boom of thunder, like cannon fire. If you are standing outside, you are drenched in seconds. These sights and sounds happen not once, not twice, but over and over. As a child, when the thunder struck, I'd grab my black and tan German Shepherd, Trigger, who was unafraid and would drag her under the bed and hug her tightly.

The large monsoon drains that run parallel and between Bukit Timah Road and Dunearn Road in Singapore are open channels, ten feet high and wide, with sides that slope in the shape of a 'V'. In a heavy downpour, these drains go from being deep, empty canyons to full to the brim with turbulent gushing, muddy water. To me, these monsoon storms were at once a terror and an exhilaration.

I turn my thoughts from the homelands that the children in Woomera Detention Centre must yearn for to the family they have left behind, drawing the comparison with my own large family, and what it would have been like to have been taken away from them at a young age.

My maternal grandfather came over to Singapore as an orphan from mainland China. His ethnicity is Hakka, originating from Northern China, and now settled in South China, mainly in the Guangdong province. The Hakka people were traditionally nomadic, and their hard-working, resilient, and modest characteristics are testament to their history.

We called my grandfather Ah Kong, in the same way Westerners call their grandmothers Nana. The name Ah Kong denotes authority and endearment in different measures. For my grandfather, the description was more of the former.

He arrived in Singapore penniless and deaf. Whenever we spoke to him we would write our conversation down, or use our own sign and body language to speak to him. His name was Chia Yee Soh. My mother told me he had a bicycle shop, and later dealt in cars and spare car parts. As he was deaf, my mother said that he could tell what was wrong with the car by turning the engine on and putting his body against the chassis, so that he could feel the vibrations. Not only was he skilled with engines, he must have been a good businessman, as during my teens I heard him being referred to as a millionaire.

He was a tall, spare man of few words, written or spoken. We grandchildren looked up to him with respect verging on fear. All his children and grandchildren obeyed him without hesitation. He began the Chia dynasty in Singapore.

He had three wives, as polygamy was allowed in those days. You have to be well-to-do to have three wives. His first wife's maiden name was Seow, but we knew her simply as Ah Mak—grandmother.

Other than her maiden name, I do not know her given names, as she was always Ah Mak to me.

Ah Mak spoke mainly Malay, with English and Cantonese as additional languages, which she spoke with equal proficiency. She was an understanding person, but could be fierce when crossed.

Ah Mak had eleven children. The eldest was my mother, Phyllis. Then came Auntie Mary, Uncle Charlie, Uncle Robert, Auntie Alice, Auntie Nellie, Auntie Elsie, Uncle Ron, Auntie Winnie, Uncle Harold and Uncle Lionel, in order of birth.

Auntie Alice was 'given away'. Ah Kong used to travel up country, driving from Singapore northwards through Malaya[3], as far as Penang. He did this, stopping at many of the major towns along the way, including Johor Bahru, Kajang, Seremban, Ipoh, Taiping, where he would stop in to see the agents for his car spare part business. One of these agents became a very good friend of Ah Kong, and was given one of Ah Kong's daughters to raise—Auntie Alice.

Another good friend of Ah Kong and Ah Mak was their family doctor, Dr Lee. Dr Lee delivered all Ah Mak's babies. As Dr Lee and her husband had no children of their own, Ah Kong and Ah Mak gave them Auntie Winnie and Uncle Lionel.

There was no nasty gossip about giving away children back then. In fact, in later years, I heard one of my uncles say he wished he had been given away to the doctor, as he would be better off than he was now.

Ah Kong's second wife was Ah Ee Poh, translated as 'second wife'. I also do not know her full name. She spoke Cantonese, with

---

[3] Malaya was a former country consisting of the Malay States and the Straits Settlements of Penang and Malacca (now Melaka). It was a British protectorate until independence in 1957. A federation formed in 1948 and it joined Malaysia in 1963.

only a very little English. She was a quiet lady, and blended in with the family. Ah Ee Poh had two children, Uncle Willie and Uncle Ah Chye.

Uncle Willie later studied medicine in Australia and became a pathologist, based in Newcastle. Uncle Ah Chye went into the family business.

Ah Kong's third wife was known as Guat Goh. We called her Poh Poh—a variation of grandmother. She had six children. They were Uncle Eric, Uncle Denis, Auntie Olive, Auntie Pearl, Auntie Irene and Auntie Eunice. In Australia, it was sometimes confusing to explain to my friends how my aunt was younger than me.

My mother did not see eye to eye with my grandfather about this relationship with his third wife. As a result, we saw very little of Poh Poh, and only began to connect with our aunts and uncles from this marriage in our adult years. I knew Uncle Denis best of all. He had the ability to communicate between all three grandmothers, and all of my nineteen aunts and uncles. It was some feat. I appreciate Uncle Denis' happy and balanced attitude.

Ah Kong's nineteen children meant that we not only had an abundance of aunts and uncles, but also a multitude of cousins. Growing up surrounded by our extended family meant that after I moved to Australia I experienced feelings of extreme loneliness and solitude. How we celebrate during Chinese New Year gives an idea of the importance of family, and the nature of our family gatherings.

Once again, my thoughts turn to how the Arabic children must have missed the celebration of their New Year at the end of Ramadan.

Our Chinese New Year depended on the lunar calendar, so that the date changed each year. When I was a child, Chinese New Year was celebrated over two weeks. It started on the eve, when there was a quiet dinner with immediate family at home. Then the big day arrived, when the most senior family member—in terms of age—had an 'open house', where guests flowed in and out of the house for the whole day, with the final visitors leaving at around nine or ten o' clock at night.

In my family, we got up early and dressed in our best before converging at the Chia mansion—Ah Kong and Ah Mak's place in Cairnhill Circle. When I say *all*, it was my nineteen aunts and uncles, their children, my parents, and my siblings. All the children and unmarried adults were given an 'ang pow'—red envelope—in which there was some money. The amount of money in the envelope was dependent on both the wealth of the giver and the fondness they had for the receiver.

On the dining tables in the mansion were all manner of delicacies. One table would be piled high with crystallised fruits, including pineapple, mango and cucumber, small pastries with sweet and nutty fillings, and Nonya cakes and biscuits. Nonya derives from a melding of Chinese and Malayan flavours.

On another table would be savoury foods such as chicken, duck, pork, beef, fish and prawns, done in spicy Chinese, Thai, Nonya, Malayan and Indian sauces.

On yet another table were all types of fizzy drinks under the trade name of Frasers and Neave, in such flavours as orange, lime, passionfruit and sarsaparilla—which was my favourite.

I don't recall any alcoholic drinks being available. Perhaps they were on another table, away from the eyes and the hands of the children. If there were alcoholic beverages, they would have included Tiger beer, brandy and whisky. Wine was not popular then. As fast as the dishes and drinks were depleted, they were replenished by the cook, Ah Niok, and the maids. Ah Niok was with my grandfather's household for as long as I could remember. He was more a family friend than an employee, and his cooking was excellent.

We would spend almost the whole day at the mansion, as different aunts, uncles and cousins would arrive and depart throughout the day. Over the next couple of days we would visit, in sequence, my paternal grandmother's place, my parents' friends and my dad's business associates. It was a great time, gathering lots of ang pows, much to our delight.

On my mother's side, my aunts and uncles were great characters, and we communicated with them frequently. I remember they were all fun to be with. They loved to gossip about the family—the good, the bad and sometimes the outright awful! I suppose it was a good experience for when I went into politics.

Phyllis, my mother, was the eldest in the family. But she was a girl, so she did not feature much in my grandfather's eyes. This did not deter her, and she led many major arguments against grandfather. She was most outspoken on any topic that she thought was not being justly debated. In a time when children were to be seen and not heard, such outbursts from my mother were unusual, unexpected and disgraceful. And from a girl, as well!

Uncle Charlie was my grandfather's eldest son. He was given all the responsibility to look after the huge family, and it has to be said that not all members of the family were easy characters. In spite of all his chores, he was a happy person who liked to dance and sing. At my teenage parties, he even danced with me—much to my embarrassment and my family's amusement. His wife, Auntie Janet, was a gracious and generous person. They had four children, Kenny, Jennifer, Chee Ming and Chee Kong.

I was closest to Kenny, as he was with us in Sydney during World War II. He was a smart, cheeky and quick-witted person. He was a successful architect, and generously supported me with a substantial donation during my political endeavours.

Auntie Mary was a big lady, and was always impeccably presented. She loved jewellery, and would never be seen without her diamonds and pearls. She was generous, and if you admired a piece of jewellery that she was wearing, she would give it to you. She was also sympathetic to our teenaged problems. Auntie Mary was great fun to be with, as she would joke with us—and when she was the butt of a joke, she would swear shockingly in Malay and Cantonese. I can't even write the swear words she would use! This brought giggles and exclamations of feigned astonishment from her nieces and nephews. Auntie Mary and my mother got on well together. Auntie Mary had three children, named Stephen, Irene and Eddie. We were not close to them, although I'm not sure why.

Uncle Robert, a tall and handsome man, was a quiet person. He was athletic and reported to be a great tennis player in his younger days. We appreciated him as a peacemaker, as with such a large family filled with such strong characters, it was inevitable that there were clashes. He lived in Penang, and we did not see much of him. My younger brother, Laurence, loved to visit him in Penang. They had long chats together, while sipping a fair amount of the golden liquor. His wife, Auntie Vivien, was a lovely, calm person and an outstanding cook—especially of Nonya food. This type of food is very time consuming to cook, and I never was able to get the recipes for her creations, as the measurements were in handfuls and pinches. Uncle Robert and Auntie Vivien had five sons, and an adopted daughter. Their names were Raymond, Mervyn, Christopher,

Jeffrey, Vincent and Corrine. I got on best with Raymond, the eldest, because he was closest to my age. He was a happy person, full of jokes, and he used to support me during strong altercations with my elders.

Auntie Nellie was a tall, athletic woman. She had many boyfriends, but never married. She was a social worker, and was always compassionate, especially towards disabled people. During World War II, she was in Perth as part of the WAAF (Women's Auxiliary Australian Airforce). She was very proud of being a member of this group, and would often tell me how useful they were during the war.

Auntie Elsie was a kind and generous person, and always had time for me. She married an Indonesian businessman called Uncle Hank and they lived in Jakarta. Unfortunately, Uncle Hank died relatively young. He and Auntie Elsie had four children called Heidi, Kris, Wendy and Jenny. Aunt Elsie and I met infrequently, but the few times we did, we seemed to have empathy for each other. I think at times she saw me as vulnerable, as she herself had been. I think she was my favourite aunt. Of her children, Kris was closest to me, as he was the eldest in the family. Kris became a very successful businessman.

Uncle Ron was gay, good-looking and an enigma. He was eloquent, and told tales and jokes which either horrified us or kept us in stitches. He also wrote well. However, he always seemed to blot his copybook by telling tales which were untrue, and which caused a lot of friction within the family. I tried to rationalise his behaviour, as he was always being stereotyped for being gay and therefore weird. However, when an untruth caused friction with my son, I was not so forgiving of his shortcomings.

Aunt Winnie was one of the aunts that was given away. She was a bohemian and lived in Melbourne. She told me she didn't care that her hippie ways outraged the more conventional members of our vast family. I agreed with her.

Uncle Lionel—the youngest of Ah Kong's first wife's children—was given away, together with Auntie Winnie, so I did not have much contact with him. However, I remembered him as softly spoken, artistic and musical. Auntie Vera was his wife, and they had five children. I did not have contact with the children.

Uncle Harold, who lives in Melbourne, was also tall and good-looking. He was an engineer; a garrulous person, intelligent and very thrifty. Auntie Hildegarde was his wife, and they had two girls, Irmgarde (Irmie) and Barbara, both of whom became doctors.

Aunt Alice was given away, and I did not know her at all.

Within this group of aunts and uncles, my mother spent most of her time with Uncle Charlie and his wife Auntie Janet, Auntie Mary, Uncle Ron, Auntie Nellie and Uncle Robert and his wife Auntie Vivien. They were the eldest members of the family, so they were closest to one another in age, but they also had a common interest in that they loved to play Mah Jong. This game is played habitually by the Chinese, and lasts the whole day, with only a break for lunch. Their games would start at 10am and end at about 5pm, when they had to go home to their families.

Mah Jong is played by four people, and the game must not need much concentration, as whenever my family got together for a game, they appeared to be able to gossip incessantly. When Mah Jong was held at my home, I could hear the clacking of the playing pieces, and the constant murmur of voices. If I happen to be studying for an exam, I found the Mah Jong group most frustrating. This may be partly why, although I know the game, I never wanted to play it.

My vast extended family did help me to understand all the bickering that happens in politics. It also provided a feeling of security and safety in numbers, as there was always someone to give you a sympathetic ear. Additionally, it gave me a greater insight and deeper compassion when looking after the Middle Eastern families in Woomera, who also tended to have large extended families.

On the other side of the family, my paternal grandmother arrived in Singapore from China as a single mum with two sons. My dad was the younger of the two. We called my father's mother 'Ah Mm' and as with my maternal grandmothers, I do not know her by any other name. Ah Mm came from the Fuzhou (Foochow) province, and spoke the Fuzhou dialect. She had very little English. As we grandchildren only spoke English, Cantonese and Malay, we had difficulty communicating with her.

She must have been a very strong person to find the drive to bring her two sons over to Singapore, as a single mother. We were never told what happened to her husband. The strain must have been considerable, as she was always very frail in health. My memory of her was that she was very grey and very thin. However, when she spoke (in Fuzhou), it was with a strong voice and great authority.

Although they were poor, my grandmother had the foresight to send my father to St Andrew's Anglican School, rather than putting him to work at an early age. It was a Chinese custom that if funds were limited, education was a priority, so you sacrificed all to send at least one child to be educated. My dad, although he was the younger of the two boys, was chosen. Dad's brother was a quiet man, and he adored my father. We called him Ah Pek. I recall the few times my father took us to visit his mother and Ah Pek's family. Due to the mess around the place, my dad always became very upset. Ah Pek used to calm the situation. Ah Pek had four sons: Ah Lek, Johnny, Seng Poh, Sonny, and one daughter, Irene, who was adopted.

I'm not sure why, but we were not close to them. However, there must have been a close bond between my father and his brother, as when my father died, Ah Pek died three months later, from no apparent physical reason.

My father qualified to become a secondary school teacher. After my father had completed his HSC exams, and the results were put on the notice board, he did not see his name. He was depressed, believing he must have failed everything. He was slowly walking away through the school corridors when the principal came out of his office and called to my dad. He told my dad that he had his results with him, and that my dad was given a special mention. My dad had topped the class with honours, and the principal wanted to congratulate him personally. My dad's name was Robert Eu Eng Wah.

When my dad married my mum, it was looked upon as him marrying above his social status. Later, my dad became a very successful and well-respected businessman. He dealt in American and Japanese cars. The American car was the Opel and the Japanese car was the Subaru, of Nissan parentage. I remember he was offered the agency of Holden from Australia, but he declined. He played the jingle for me, "Holding you in my Holden…Life is completely sublime…"

He built up a car sales agency from scratch, called Singapore Motors Ltd.

I recall that anytime he saw an Opel car stalled on the roadside, he would stop our car, even with mother and us children inside the car, no matter where we were heading, to make sure that the owner was given help. He not only sold cars, he made sure the customers were satisfied. That was the secret of his success. I have taken that policy of patient satisfaction into my practice of medicine.

Dad soon was able to move from the house that my Ah Kong gave my mother as a wedding present to a larger place, and to put my older brother and I through university abroad, and my younger brother through the University of Malaya.

My mother was a strong and ambitious woman. Her name was Phyllis Eu, née Chia. She was, as mentioned, the first of eleven children, and I understand that Ah Kong admired her forthright attitude, in spite of the fact that they had many strong and frank arguments.

She was a very busy person, as she was a full-time teacher, majoring in high school English. She later became a full-time politician of the Singapore City Council, which was partly under the British, and she later returned to school as the full-time principal of the Paya Lebar Methodist Girls' School.

During her time as a politician, I recalled slogans for her such as "Grow More Food" and "I love Eu". She certainly did a lot for the community. However, as she was very busy with politics, something had to give, and that something was bonding with her children.

Father was also busy building up a business for us, and so we did not spend much time with our parents. We had help from maids. We had special ones known as the "black and whites", as they were dressed in white tops fashioned with a high Chinese collar and Chinese buttons, and loose cut black trousers. They were called "ahmahs", and different from the usual maids. Ahmahs are single and live as part of the family. When our mother went overseas for conferences, we were not overly worried, but when our ahmahs left to visit family in China, we would bawl our eyes out.

In contrast, the 200 or so children in the Woomera Detention Centre have only their parents, who are constantly stressed with fear and anger as they wait unendingly for a decision as to whether they can stay in Australia. The parents let their young children wander around the centre, unsupervised, and stay up late at night, so that in the morning they were too tired to go to the makeshift school. The parents were disinterested and lethargic, which are signs of depression.

Not only was the environment chaotic, but the parents were stumbling.

Stumbling parents are better than no parents at all, though. Recently, there have been reports that children of asylum seekers might be separated from their parents.

This would be a disaster.

**

I have two brothers, my elder brother, Leslie, is a year older than me, and my younger brother, Laurence, is ten years younger. The gap in age between my younger brother and me was due to the war. When Japan joined the war in 1940, my family's women and children were sent to Sydney, while the men stayed in Singapore. My parents did not see each other until the end of the war, in 1945.

Because Leslie was the eldest male child of the family, it was very difficult to criticise him. This was a Chinese custom imbued in us from childhood. When my father died at the relatively young age of 54, Leslie took over the family car business. As he had a gambling addiction, he was not able to run the business properly.

In line with our Chinese custom, we were not able to speak out against our eldest brother. It was a shame that my brother had this addiction, as he was an intelligent person. He was able to write beautiful prose, and he had the gift of the gab.

The addiction was a flaw or a disease that impacted not only on him, but devastated the whole family. So, unfortunately, with money leaking out from my brother's gambling, my father's business, Singapore Motor Ltd., was brought to an inevitable demise.

I have always been close to my younger brother Laurence, and supported him as much as possible. As he was ten years younger, I looked after him frequently with the ahmah, helping to bring him up. I admire his fortitude, as he had to run the family business together with his flawed older brother. I never heard that he uttered a word of recrimination or of denunciation of his older brother to anyone.

As for myself, after completing high school, I was in Australia, and even had I been in Singapore, I was not business orientated, although perhaps I could have given moral support to Laurence.

In the Woomera Detention Centre, I do not recall much or even any children's laughter. It is a sad place. I cannot help but equate it with sorrow—such a vast difference between my happy teenage years and the misery of the children in the detention centre.

During my school days at the Methodist Girls' School, every Friday morning, dressed in our white blouses with an 'MGS' brooch clipped to the front edge of the sailor collars, and our starched, pleated, navy-blue skirts, we would gather in the assembly hall and sing hymns, mainly written by John Wesley.

Our classmate, Helen, would be at the piano, and without a teacher in sight, we would shout out what hymn we wanted to sing, such as, 'Onward Christian soldiers', 'What a friend we have in Jesus', 'All things bright and beautiful', 'Just as I am', and many others.

The place where we would assemble was a large hall with doors open at either side, and the rich and soaring songs filled not only the hall but the whole of the school.

Our singing teacher, Mrs Elsie Lyne, a gentle Englishwoman, would come in towards the end of our assembly and congratulate us for being able to carry on without her. Mrs Lyne was also in charge of the Girls' Life Brigade, of which I was a member. The Girls' Life Brigade was similar to Girl Guides.

Of special, happy recollection, is the memory of a group of four or five carefree girls heading out at the end of the school day with Helen, the daughter of the principal, in her black open-roofed car with her Malay driver, Dollah, to tour around Singapore. We did this about once week, and always greatly looked forward to the outing. We were around 14 to 15 years of age at the time.

The girls were Boung Gee, Tiong, Choo, Helen and myself.

In the car, our Singlish goes like this, "Where shall we go, lah?" Giggle, giggle.

"Don't know, lah, let's eat something!"

"Where to, man, to Koek Lane or Bras Basah Road?"

"OK, lah. First go to Koek Lane to eat char siew korn low mee (roast pork with mixed dry noodles) and after we go to Bras Basah, lah."

"What for we go to Bras Basah, lah?"

"Eat curry puff and ice kacang, lah. You don't know?" Giggle, giggle.

Of our little group, Helen, being the principal's daughter, had special privileges.

If it was raining, and it can be heavy as described, Mrs Handy would have her driver, Dollah, come to the class with an umbrella and take Helen to the car.

We accepted it as the done thing, but after being educated in Australia, we would poke fun at Helen for what would now be perceived as an unacceptable privilege. Helen also came to Adelaide to study medicine. She was Eurasian, and an easygoing person, in spite of the fact that she was the principal's daughter.

She was taller than most of us and was into all the activities we concocted. She played the piano beautifully. The rest of us were Chinese-looking, and although Helen looked European, there was not an iota of consciousness that she was different. Not forgetting that we knew each other since we were five years old.

Boung Gee was our reporter, as she had the knack of obtaining and remembering news of our friends and foes. She also came to Adelaide to study medicine. She was the most physically curvaceous of us all, and this was much appreciated in our Western university environment. Tiong Choo was a jolly and carefree girl, with a beautiful singing voice. She studied food science and, having married a New Zealander, emigrated to New Zealand, after which we lost touch with her. There were another six MGS girls who have kept in touch from primary one until today.

Briefly, there is Letty, the spiritual one—a most generous person and the one to go to when you require an opinion. She also studied medicine. Poh Tin is the elegant one—a great cook—as she should be, as she studied what was then called domestic science. She had an aura of graciousness and provided serenity to our group. Eileen was the smart and practical one. She was community-minded and involved in numerous local, government and professional groups. She also studied medicine. Biau Hee was the accommodating one. An arts graduate, she taught secondary students. Suat Hoon was the helpful one. She would go to great lengths to provide exceptional hospitality. She was a doctor, and passed away some years ago, after she became infected with SARS while nursing her son during the epidemic. Alice, the eccentric one, did exactly what she wanted. We are now seven, as three of us have passed away. And what of me? I am told that I am the determined one. This rich and varied life makes me wonder if the asylum seekers miss their former life as much as I missed mine.

From left: Laurence, younger brother; Myself; Leslie, older brother.

Mum & Dad.

Dad.

Myself.

From left: Leslie, Dad, Mum, baby Laurence, Myself.

Mum & Myself

CHAPTER 8

Love

Growing up in Singapore and attending a same-sex school until after completing my Leaving Certificate left me with very little experience of the opposite sex. When I had to complete my Higher School Certificate, a group of us from the Methodist Girls' School went to our brother school, the Anglo Chinese School, as our school did not have the higher science subjects required to do medicine, such as chemistry, physics, and biology or additional mathematics, such as algebra and geometry. The assumption in those days seemed to be that women did not study medicine.

It was the first time that our group mixed with boys on a daily basis.

It was a very interesting and enjoyable time, as we were surrounded by boys, all of whom were on their best behaviour. A small group of boys would come over to our desks to chat every morning. They would also offer to sharpen our pencils. We found it hard to concentrate on our subjects.

The main perceptions of love and romance that we had had come from the movies. Of course, it was Hollywood style and everything ended happily ever after. When Doris Day married, it ended with her being carried into the bedroom and the door closing. As a result, I had a very romantic view of boy–girl relationships. Our greatest displays of affection was holding hands and cuddling. I recall a scripture lesson at school, when the teacher, a visiting American missionary called Miss Gruber, asked, "Who can tell me the greatest love story in the Bible?"

My hand shot up.

"Yes. Bernice?"

"Samson and Delilah!" I responded enthusiastically, having just seen the glorious Technicolor MGM blockbuster.

"No! Certainly not! It's Ruth and Naomi!"

What? I thought, *Who are they?* I was about to contradict her, but shut my mouth when I was given a withering stare.

You can appreciate the culture shock when we arrived in Adelaide!

We thought—or at least *I* thought—that kissing could get you pregnant. And I was 16 or 17 years of age at the time. Furthermore, the day I started my menstrual period, I thought I was dying, with all this blood coming out of my body.

How different is it now? When I was recently bathing my granddaughter, Scarlett, I said, "I want to wash your bum and your boom-boom."

She replied, "You mean my bum and my vagina, Nana?"

She was all of six years old.

In the sixth and final year of my medical course, I met the man I was to marry. He was in his fifth year of medicine, and his name was John. He was tall and good-looking—my criteria for a great guy—with light brown eyes and messy fair hair. Our courting days were simple. My Asian girl friends were agog, as I was one of the few Asians that had a serious relationship with a white Aussie. They wanted to know where he took me to dinner. I said we had hot dogs.

"Ahyah!" they responded, "Why not a nice Chinese restaurant?"

"He hasn't much money," I defended. They thought that he was tight.

Meanwhile, my parents were aware that I had met a white Australian, and that I liked him. This information caused a furore among my large extended family.

"Why would you want to marry an *ang mow guiah* (red-haired devil), lah?" The asked in dismay.

Older members of the family added, "They do nothing but drink beer every day, until they vomit! Ahyah, Bernice!"

My response, "But he is a good one, and studying to be a doctor."

"A white Australian doctor also drink lot, lah! Why you don't marry your dad's rich business friend's son, lah?" they complained.

And so I was called back to do the second part of my internship at the Kandang Kerbau Hospital, Singapore.

In Singapore, apart from being overwhelmed with the medical work in the Kandang Kerbau Hospital, I was overcome with the many young men who were introduced to me. As you know, the harder you are pushed one way, the more you want to push the other way.

Doggedly, I applied to return to Australia, but my visa seemed to take a long time to come through. Unbeknownst to me, my parents had got in touch with the Australian Embassy in Singapore to prevent, or at least delay, the issuing of my visa.

I communicated directly to the Royal Adelaide Hospital to obtain a job as a second-year intern, in the Casualty Department. My application was snapped up, as casualty was not a popular specialty at that time. However, John and I wanted to be reunited as soon as possible. So whatever job would provide me with a quick visa was good, which is why I had chosen casualty.

Finally, I obtained my visa, and was on my way back to Adelaide, and to John.

He met me at the airport in his crumpled pants and shirt, with arms outstretched and an Esky full of all types of drinks. Off we went for a picnic, where he gave me an engagement present—a pair of square opal earrings, set in a filigree silver design. I was so touched. I still have them.

We didn't want a big wedding. We knew that my parents would object, as they considered him foreign, and that the cultural differences would be too difficult for them and me to understand and overcome. His parents would not be too fussed, he said.

In the end it seemed too hard, and we decided that we would go to the registry office to be married, and tell both sets of parents after. This we did.

We went on a short honeymoon to the Flinders Ranges, and decided to tell our parents after we returned. The honeymoon was a unique experience. Firstly, John decided that we should go camping, and that he would shoot our tucker. He would bring some flour to make a damper, and an Esky for our wine. I guess I was too much in love to query if this was a good idea. So off we went to the Flinders Ranges.

The Flinders Ranges are a chain of rugged mountains at the heart of the Flinders Ranges National Park, about 200 kilometres north of Adelaide. Part of the ranges forms a sickle-shaped natural amphitheatre, known as Wilpena Pound, stretching for about 400 kilometres. The rocks there are 630 million years old, and fossils can be found embedded in the rock. There are amazing gorges and abundant wildlife, with kangaroos and emus. The ancient site's Traditional Owners are the Adnyamathanha people. The colours of desk. He was fast asleep. I understand that RMOs now have better hours.

John and I had very little time together in the first two years of married life. Not only were we working hard as RMOs, we also bought a house that needed renovating, so whatever spare time we had together, we were busy doing home repairs. We forgot to find time just to relax.

After the two years of John's internship were completed, we made the traditional trip over to the United Kingdom, via Singapore, Thailand, India, Europe and London. We stopped for some time in Singapore, and I worked on a research project at my previous obstetrics and gynaecological hospital, the Kandang Kerbau Hospital, while John worked in Johor Bahru, Malaya, at the general hospital.

It was a good experience, especially the opportunity to introduce John to Asian food.

In particular, our durian fruit served to show us the way. This tropical fruit is the size of an Australian Rules football. It is just as hard, but heavier, and green and covered in sharp sturdy spikes. While the look of it is not that great, it is the smell that provokes the sharpest censure. To open the durian fruit is quite a difficult manoeuvre, but once opened, apart from the smell, it is rather beautiful. Each side is divided by a pearly white fibrous skin, and in the pouches formed there sit creamy, glistening, yellow pods. However, to eat it has been described as eating custard while sitting on a full toilet. This fruit is banned from hotels and from airplanes. It once caused my father's Japanese client to excuse himself from my father's car and catch a taxi—with the greatest of apologies.

John found it to be 'an acquired taste'. In Johor Bahru, where

John was working, and which is arguably a hot spot for durians, his fellow medicos were mad for durians. As it was durian season, they ordered the fruit by the basketful. He declared that if he had some brandy and then the durian, he could cope with the smell.

This combination of durian and brandy was greeted with some consternation, as it was folklore that if you did this, you would die. John declared it to be a myth. So with the brandy to smother the smell, he ate the durian. He did not die. He now loves durian.

When we finally arrived in London, we had a tough time getting jobs, as we hadn't thought to get references from our previous jobs in Adelaide. We stayed in London for eight years. John did his specialist degree in anaesthetics. I did not specialise, as our two children, Lian and Rob, arrived, and one parent had to do the child rearing. We soon returned to Adelaide, as with its many parks, gardens, beaches and sunshine, it was more conducive to bringing up children than the bleak, dark and cold climate of London. But London, except for its weather, is a wonderful place. The history, the art galleries, the music, the theatres and the closeness of European and the Middle Eastern countries, all filled in the cultural gap that faraway Australia lacked, and contributed to our understanding of those immigrants who came to our shores and called Australia the Antipodes.

In Adelaide, I worked in child development, employed in a well-baby clinic known as the Mothers' and Babies' Health Association. I was able to work normal office hours, instead of medical hours, which invariably involve working at weekends and being on call. Being married to a doctor, it must be said that you are like a single mum, as John's hours were five days a week, alternate weekends and being on call. John was busy with his career and his research. I missed my extended family, who would have helped out.

As relaxation, I liked to cook Nonya food. This type of food is seldom available in restaurants, and if it were, it would not be authentic. I cooked for our group of medical colleagues and their wives. They were Chris and Rosemary, Con and Mary, Erik and Mary, Ossie and Rayena, and us.

I would cook and they would bring the wine. Apart from the food and wine, it was a group where we could share topics of any shade, without worrying about what we were saying under the influence. I also was happy watching how all enjoyed the food. This would happen about once a month. I do miss this gathering.

John and I didn't make time for ourselves.

We drifted.

In Singapore, with preschool children, there was extended family and a maid to help. In Australia, we only had occasional help from John's parents and grandma. This put stress on the relationship, as there was hardly any time for us to go out and relax together. It makes it harder when both parents work, and one parent has to look after the children most of the time. It is important to find time to be together, as a couple, in order to keep a relationship strong.

We were both very hard-working, not only when it came to our jobs, but also with all sorts of extracurricular activities—John with his outdoor hobby of the vineyard, and I with women's groups and politics. We also made time for our children. They never had any difficulty with schoolwork or friendships. We ran a netball team for our daughter, based at her primary school. At one stage we even won a premiership for their age group. I also tried to help with Rob's football, but my kicking was not up to the Australian Rules football standard!

In amongst all of this, we overlooked having time for ourselves.

We soon had more of our own interests, which were not shared.

We drifted further apart.

My children are now adults with spouses and careers of their own. Although they are very busy with their professional lives, they make sure they have quality time with their partners.

CHAPTER 9

A Refugee

In the Woomera Detention Centre, the asylum seekers are waiting for their Temporary Protection Visa—the first step to being released, with limited freedom. The step after this is to be allowed to apply to stay in Australia as a resident, after which the golden goal is to become an Australian citizen.

In Oday's words, voiced to me in hushed tones, "Forever freedom."

There is a rigmarole to obtaining that essential first step of the Temporary Protection Visa. It helps to recall the well-known Chinese saying: *The journey of a thousand miles starts with a single step.*

At the Woomera Detention Centre, Oday is the only person I encounter with sufficient English for me to talk to about the complexities of obtaining a TPV. I direct my efforts towards helping him obtain his TPV as a first step to understanding the whole system.

As Oday had to flee from the Saddam regime of Iraq after his father was poisoned for dissenting to the policies of Saddam, and it was known that Oday shared his father's view, he is a refugee according to the UN 1951 Refugee Convention and its 1967 Protocol.

However, the Australian government is not convinced of Oday's assertions. He could be a spy. I am initially just as cautious, as I have noted that there are many asylum seekers who have come for financial improvement. They tell me as much.

I am acutely vigilant in the Woomera Detention Centre, which is a tough place. However, Oday is always consistent with his story and his behaviour. Even during the tense moments of the centre riots, or during strained counselling sessions when I monitor him closely, there is no conflict of historical facts or inconsistent behaviour. Even so, it takes me some time to be convinced that his claims are authentic.

At one counselling session, he appears to be particularly upset. I discover that he has had a call from his wife and she wants to leave him, as she could not understand why it would take so long for him to be accepted by Australia. I offered to speak to her, to explain his situation. So, through an interpreter, over a mobile phone, I explain to her that it is difficult in Australia and that she should wait, as Oday is trying his best to get his special visa. I must not have convinced her, as she left him soon after.

Another time, when I happened to visit a sick Iraqi in his donga, I bumped into Oday, as his donga was nearby. He asked me whether I wanted a cup of tea. I accepted. He brought me a cup of hot tea with milk, with a folded tissue serving as a saucer. I was touched.

Another time, Oday appeared at the medical clinic with a gift. It was a rustic but beautiful plaque crafted by Oday on behalf of the Woomera asylum seekers. Oday presented it to me as their delegate.

The plaque was made from chipboard, painted black with a silver border, upon which was mounted an impressionistic figure of Hammurabi, King of Babylon. The figure was made of metal pieces, cut out painstakingly by hand with a piece of sharp stone, and arranged with royalty in mind—the king was mounted in a conspicuous position. Sharp objects like scissors were not allowed. The effort that had gone into making this plaque took my breath away, and washed the myriad hassles of the day from my tired mind. I accepted with humility.

Oday's plaque.

There were three factors at that time that had to be ratified before a TPV could be granted. Those three factors were being a refugee specifically, as opposed to an asylum seeker. An asylum seeker is a generic term that includes not only refugees but also economic migrants and those seeking a better life without fear of their safety in their homeland. The second factor was being of good character, and thirdly was being in good health.

The Refugee Convention was adopted at the United Nations Conference in 1951 and became legally binding in 1954. The Convention is the main international legal document relating to refugee protection, and initially applied only to people affected by World War II.

In 1967, the Protocol relating to the Status of Refugees removed this limitation. The Protocol is legally binding, and defines a refugee as a person who has a well-founded fear of persecution for reasons of race, religion, nationality, membership of particular social groups or political opinion.

Under Article 33 of the Refugee Convention, a refugee cannot be sent to a place where they may be persecuted, known as 'non-refoulment'.

Under Article 31 of the Convention, countries who have signed the Convention cannot punish refugees for entering their nation or living without permission, or unnecessarily restrict their freedom of movement. The Refugee Convention recognises that refugees often need to enter a country without permission, or with false documents, in order to obtain protection.

The Office of the United Nations High Commissioner for Refugees is a United Nations program with the mandate to protect refugees, forcibly displaced communities and stateless people, and assist in their voluntary repatriation, local integration or resettlement to a third country.

The United Nations High Commission for Refugee (UNHCR) is the guardian agency for monitoring the implementation of the 1951 Refugee Convention and its extension in the 1967 Protocol, relating to the status of refugee.

Australia was one of the first countries to become a party to the

1951 Refugee Convention in 1954, and later became a party to the 1967 Protocol, in 1973.

As I had previously been in politics, I made an appointment to see the Minister of Immigration, Mr Phillip Ruddock, to try to convince him that Oday's statements were bona fide. My attempts were unsuccessful.

Later, Oday informs me that there is a family from Tikrit who had escaped to England, and that he could get their contact details. I agree that it is worth pursuing, and contact is made. It proves to be a most effective move, as the family are anti-Saddam, and well known in England.

I send faxes back and forth to the family, requesting that they confirm Oday's anti-Saddam sentiments, and the poisoning of his father. Thankfully, we get the confirmation we need. Phillip Ruddock is finally convinced.

We then hope that the refugee status will be ratified.

The next factor is that of being of 'good character'. This was, to our minds, something that should not have been a problem. Oday had a clean sheet in terms of criminality, and he was an upright person within the community of the detention centre. We shared how he offered his translation abilities, how he helped others and how the asylum seekers in the Woomera Detention Centre vouched for his integrity.

This assessment had to go through ASIO, the Australian Security Intelligence Organisation. We did not hear anything for many weeks. After this time, I engaged a lawyer to progress the application for the Temporary Protection Visa. Several months later, the lawyer said that the application was either still with ASIO or on the minister's desk. I wrote to ASIO three times, and had two replies that they had not found anything negative when checking into Oday's character. Indeed, the letter from ASIO said they had cleared him three times. The letters must have been on the minister's desk!

The problem is that these confirmations of good character and eligibility for refugee status only last a set time, and we were chasing our tails. When one status became valid, the other status expired.

We then found that we needed to apply to the AAT, the Administrative Appeals Tribunal. All these applications were done on the supposition that it was the correct way to go, with no help from the Department of Immigration or from anybody else who should have known. Even our private lawyer could only guess what needed to be done, and speculate about what the holdups might be.

Finally, we received a request to attend the Administrative Appeals Tribunal, to appeal against Oday being held under administrative detention, in accordance with Article 31, relating to refugees being unlawfully detained in the country of refuge.

A distinction to make here is to assess whether the detention is for the purpose of carrying out a thorough investigation—such as ascertaining whether the individual is of good character—versus imposing penalties for illegal entry, which is disallowed where entry is justified.

I engaged a lawyer friend, Peter Waye, to defend Oday. He worked pro bono. We also asked one of Oday's close friends to be witness for his good character. We were unable to urge another friend of Oday's to bear witness, as he had been a refugee and was now in an influential position in Adelaide. He did not want to rock the boat. This type of position infuriates me, and I told him so. He was not impressed, and threatened to report me. I was also a witness.

With the excellent defence of Peter Waye, supportive evidence made while in detention, but all of the people who had recently been released had problems of their own.

I tried to lift his spirits through travel around Australia, showing him the vastness, the dryness and the uniqueness that is Australia.

He said, "My country very beautiful too, but all fighting!"

"When will it stop?" I asked.

"When no more blood to give," came the reply.

The people he met surprised him with their friendly and welcoming attitudes. The only Australians he has had significant exposure to at Woomera Detention Centre were the guards, who were impersonal at best, and unfriendly and belligerent at worst.

"I can't believe that Australians are so kind," he remarked with pleasure and surprise.

I accompanied him to Perth, where he agreed to support the Federal Police in a court case identifying a person who was involved in the illegal trafficking of asylum seekers to Australia from Indonesia.

He is a gentle soul, and loves children in particular, always stopping to play or talk to them. I tell him that he can't talk to kids he does not know.

"Why?" he asks in amazement!

Once I took him to Hahndorf, for an Aussie picnic, with gourmet pies, German sausages, fresh-baked bread and wine. Coming from a Muslim country, the wine was new to him. Unexpectedly, he looked unhappy—cross, even. We had an uncomfortable lunch. At a later date, when we were at a posh but stiff lunch at a French restaurant, he said to me, "You remember the picnic we had together? I love that more."

"Really, you didn't show it then!" I replied.

"I not know. I think you give me rubbish food, and sit outside in rubbish place. I think you give me no respect. But I now know that it is very good, Australian way."

He hugged me!

Differences in cultures can be an obstacle to a harmonious relationship. There were numerous such instances. Especially when his self-esteem was at an all-time low. When he perceived a tone of disrespect, his reaction became aggressive and belligerent, which was quite out of character for the person.

We got to know each other better, in spite of the cultural differences. We had warm intentions towards each other. Except for the occasional cultural and self-esteem clashes, he was appreciative of the help given, and I appreciated the care he gave and had for me.

Once, he gave me a single rose. He said that all the men at the florist were buying roses, so he bought one too, although it was clear he didn't understand the significance. It was February the 14th—Valentine's Day.

This warmth was generated through care for each other, and the closeness that hard lobbying and many failures bring. The lobbying for the Temporary Protection Visa, and later for Permanent Residency, brought an indescribable bond. I had not felt this way for a long time. The feeling of being wanted, of being constantly included, of being given little gifts for no apparent reason. Being touched with great warmth was overwhelming as we hugged each other. His hugs are special. It is not just the arms around shoulders pressure. It is an all-out tight embrace, which takes your breath away, and you are embarrassed that all eyes are on you.

So, guilty as I felt, I did not stop this building emotion between the both of us.

Love intervened.

John and I separated, and then divorced.

Things flashed by quickly. Oday and I got married, the Permanent Residency was granted, and citizenship could not be granted rapidly enough. Finally, Oday became a citizen of Australia. Looking at his happy face, I believe it was the proudest day of his life! We hugged and drank champagne.

We went to Singapore and I introduced him to my family. They were a bit unsure about him. We went to London and saw my son Rob, and Alissa, my daughter-in-law. They accepted him because I did. We travelled through mainland Europe, as Oday had never been out of Iraq, other than when he made the journey to Australia, and I am a big believer that travel broadens the mind.

When we returned to Adelaide, Oday enrolled in an English class for professionals. He then applied, and was accepted into, a Masters in Health Administration course. After completing the course, was accepted for a management position at Sydney South West Area Health Service[4]. He worked long hours in the management position, and discovered the misery of being in a traffic jam on the M4 during his daily commute.

He had arrived.

---

[4] A health service now commonly known as Sydney South West Health.

CHAPTER 10

Politics

While working towards the Temporary Protection Visa for Oday, I lobbied some of my federal colleagues.

How did I get into politics?

By the mid-1980s my children had become more independent, and I had more time to relax and watch television. I noticed on a federal parliament television program that there were not many women, and no Asian faces to be seen at all.

I have always been interested in politics. Even as a young teenager, I was fascinated by mother's campaign for a Singapore City Council seat, and loved helping out wherever I could. The atmosphere was electric. The phone was ringing all the time, and people were asking what she stood for. One of her goals was to fight for women's voting rights. She called the British municipal laws, which limited women from voting, 'absurd'. My mum's slogan provided an additional answer to her goals—GROW MORE FOOD!

What does a woman know about politics? Shouldn't she be looking after the children? She is a teacher with a rich husband, what does she know about poor people? These were some of the questions I heard at the time. I cringed.

In spite of these negative attitudes, my mother was the first woman to be elected as a Member of the City Council of Singapore, under the English. Later, when the English moved towards an independent Singapore, my mother was elected as a Member of the Legislative Council, with the Presiding Member still being a person nominated by the English colonial powers.

When it came to my campaign for my mother, I was rushing around photocopying, stuffing election letters into envelopes, licking stamps, and, above all, listening to the chorus of questions and answers. I thought it was fascinating. We are really representing the community! That was my perception of what being a politician entailed.

I was elected local government councillor in, what was then known as the District Council of East Torrens of South Australia. At that time, East Torrens had an urban metropolitan area known as the Hills Face Zone, and the South Australian Parliament passed legislation to protect this area from urban development. I lived in the Hills Face Zone, and we enjoyed being close to the city while benefitting from the open spaces of the rural setting. However, there was conflict in the council. Those living in the urban area of the Hills Face Zone enjoyed the open spaces, and wanted to keep it that way. While those living in the rural area of the Hills Face Zone wanted to have the ability to subdivide their large land holdings if they chose to do so in the future. There were many uncomfortable council meetings, when full and robust debates about the benefits and drawbacks of subdivision ran late into the evenings. Most of the time, the motions to prevent further subdivision were passed by only one vote. We were called 'greenies', and would have to make sure all of us were on deck when an important motion relating to possible subdivision came on the agenda. I dreaded those evenings, as they were so combative and hostile.

When there was a subdivision motion, the mayor would say, "I suppose we have our same group voting against," and there would be murmurs from the audience.

Recently, I was happy to read an abstract online entitled 'These enchanted hills'[5] which says, "...evidence for the evolution of this landscape illustrate the dichotomies between these changing landscape values and growing public appreciation of the aesthetic qualities of this 'green' backdrop to the city of Adelaide."

'So it was worth all that intense debate, many long years ago,' I mused.

That was the first time I understood what being political meant—or so I thought. You do not make friends all around, but you make a dream for the future.

I then tried for the mayoral position of the District Council of East Torrens, but was not successful. The mayor at that time was Mayor Isabel Bishop. I found her hard-working, friendly and inclusive, even though she took the other side with regard to the subdivision. She was very fair and encouraging.

I then joined the Liberal Party of South Australia. As a rookie, they gave me the unwinnable state seat in the Port Adelaide area, needing a large sixteen percent swing to win. Of course, I was not elected. I did work the area as though there was a chance, and I think some in the Liberal Party were appreciative of my efforts.

The next time I stood was in 1990, when a sitting Member of the Legislative Council vacated his seat after a two-year sojourn of an eight-year term. I believe there were around five or six nominees for the position.

---

[5] Pamela Smith et al. (2020) 'These enchanted hills', *Landscape Research*, 45(8).

It was a tall order to nominate for that position, as it was a very sought-after position. You had to convince over two hundred delegates that you were the one. These 200 delegates lived throughout the state of South Australia. Usually there would be letters sent out to all the delegates, with a follow up phone call to all—or at least to the ones you thought might be favourable towards you. As I made my rounds, visiting the delegates, I was made aware that some delegates who did not support a particular person would try to hold them up. To detain you, they would talk incessantly about irrelevant issues, or they would make you wait as they pretended to be busy on the phone. The intention of these tactics was to waste the candidate's time, so they may miss out on going to see other delegates who might be sitting on the fence, and where a visit might convince that delegate to support you.

What were my chances, as an Asian female who had only been a member of the Liberal Party for a relatively short time? Some may also say that being a doctor could be a disadvantage.

Realising that I had a few chips stacked against me, I decided to visit all the delegates—even the delegates residing in remote rural areas. My son, Rob, came with me to the rural areas. He was in his early teens, and I believe his presence was part of the reason that some of the delegates approved of me. They would ask him questions about whether or not he read the Bible, why he came with his mum, and what he thought of my going into politics. Perhaps they were pleased with his responses. I never got around to asking him what his responses were, and, like most teenagers, he never gave me crucial information unless I asked specifically.

Most of the delegates were in the metropolitan and inner regional areas, while others were in the remote rural areas. It took twice as long visiting the remote rural delegates, and I saw half as many delegates. Most of the delegates were surprised by my personal visits, but appreciative. It was worth these visits, as the delegates in the two different areas had different issues.

On the fateful night of the 1990 election for the position in the Legislative Council in South Australia, each nominee had to give a speech, and then questions were put to each of us. I was very nervous, facing around 280 delegates and other attendees. I recall that I clasped both my hands and placed them upon the pulpit, as I had been instructed to do in speech training, and said, "I have a dream…"

The voting was by proportional representation, meaning that unless you were an outright winner, with at least fifty percent plus one vote, then voting continued until someone *was* the outright winner. On that night the voting was protracted. We started at around 6pm, and an outright winner was not declared until around midnight.

I was that winner.

What a surprise! A joy! An exhilaration! It was unbelievable. I was humbled to think I was voted to represent the people of South Australia.

I naively thought that working on behalf of the South Australian people for a better world was the main objective. Little did I know that representing the people is only part of a politician's work. Other factors, such as getting re-elected in three years' time, were apparently more important. I was informed that being *pragmatic* was the ideal.

When it became known that I had been elected to the South Australian Legislative Council, or Upper House, there were members of the media wanting to make contact. Suddenly, there was also the rumour that I was not a financial member of the Liberal Party and therefore unauthorised to stand for the position. This was, of course, totally inaccurate. But it was stressful, as the media hounded me, wanting to know 'the truth'.

Up until that point, I'd had very little experience with the media. Not even as a local council member. However, my medical background helped me respond using my common sense, while my experience as a doctor dealing with the community also helped.

When asked what I intended to do as a politician, I answered, "Represent the people of South Australia."

I understood that my position in the Legislative Council had been made vacant due to the previous member in that position being unhappy with the party. I did not know the reason. So when asked how I felt about the person who had vacated the position I now occupied, I answered that, "If I were he, I would not be very happy."

When I entered Parliament House, I felt that it was a vast, unfriendly, unknown, cold place. There wasn't anyone to show me around. I wasn't astute enough to ask a senior person where everything was. I had to hit the ground running. The trouble was I didn't know which direction to run in. I suppose most people assumed that I knew the area, but I, unlike many other candidates, had not visited Parliament House as frequently. I was fully involved in being a medical doctor, caring for patients, listening to their concerns, making a diagnosis, and either alleviating or eliminating illness. So as a true rookie to politics, I had a lot to learn.

At one stage, a tall, intimidating heavy-set man, a senior member of the House of Assembly, asked me to take a look at his prized animal photos. The photos were of bulls with their prominent genitals showing.

"Aren't you impressed?" he asked.

"You know I'm a doctor, not a vet?" I replied matter-of-factly.

"Oh. No," he responded, clearly deflated that his attempts to embarrass me had failed.

I was informed later that he was well-known for these types of interactions with female newcomers.

When I entered parliament, I became the first Asian person appointed to the Legislative Council of South Australia. There were two Members who were very supportive and encouraging. The rest in the Upper House were either lukewarm to my presence or positively negative towards me. One member even tried to block me from asking a question during Parliamentary Question Time. It is no wonder that women are reluctant to step up to take part in parliament, and no wonder climbing the ladder is so slippery.

Being a medical doctor appeared to be a negative, as whenever I made medical suggestions, it was seen as, *'She wants to be Minister of Health'*. As a rookie, that was the furthest thing from my mind.

My mother often said to me, in relation to getting a husband, that I must not show my competence else I will frighten them away. At that time, I dismissed such an idea with disdain, but now consider it possible. Competition is said to be good, as you get the best product or person. It seems in politics, competition is too threatening.

During the six years that I served in the state parliament, between 1990 to 1996, there were an extraordinary and astonishing number of changes of leadership in our party. When I came into parliament, the Labor Party was in power, and on the first day of my sitting in parliament, I shook hands with most of the Members in the Legislative Council, both Labor and Liberal. I clearly remember that I shook the hand of Premier John Bannon, from the Labor Party. He appeared sincere in welcoming me. However, with the State Bank of South Australia debacle, he did not last long. But back to the Liberal Party leadership.

Initially, on entering parliament, John Olsen was leaving as opposition leader and Dale Baker was replacing him. Then Dean Brown came in as premier. I thought he was doing well, but then there was a big internal commotion, with people rushing around, frantically looking for rooms to have meetings. One afternoon, a group of senior members descended upon me as I was having a community gathering in one of those rooms. Then, suddenly, Dean Brown was gone and John Olsen re-entered. Somehow, Graham Ingerson, then Deputy Premier, was involved. To my mind, it was disgraceful.

Joint party meetings of the Liberal Party were always an education. These meetings were enlightening and fascinating, yet shocking. The meetings were a time when the Upper House—the Legislative Council—and the Lower House—the House of Assembly—gathered around a long table, with the Premier on one side with his ministers and the other Members of the Assembly, and then the Members of the Legislative Council along the other side. The pecking order was the Premier and his ministers from the Assembly, ministers from the Legislative Council, the rest of the Members of the Assembly, and the Members of the Legislative Council. As the rookie of the Legislative Council, I didn't have very prominent seating.

When we debated any item that had medical content, I felt I knew a bit about such things and spoke out. I also spoke out on issues I was passionate about, including children's issues, ethnic issues and environmental issues. Whenever I indicated that I wanted to speak, there was a silence. I interpreted this as, *What does she want say now? Doesn't she know she should just listen?*

I felt I was back in my Asian home culture, and that the expectation was that I should be seen but not heard. This, of course, was intended to intimidate, but I felt that I had to do my part to represent the people. I continued to speak my piece. Often, a further obstructive ploy was to say, "Can you speak up? I can't hear." I would oblige, and continue to speak, and interject, if necessary. It wasn't easy going.

I began to realise that I had become more assertive and more challenging, to the point that I must have overcompensated. So much so that when my husband John and I were having a robust discussion, he'd say, "Politicians never say they are wrong."

I never thought I was that way inclined.

Also, my son not infrequently said to me that I tended to talk over people. I think he was right, as, in the beginning, I found that I could not get a word in during party debates. If I waited for my turn, it would never come. Politeness was seen as weakness. Rob also told me that I sometimes put the phone down before he or his friends had finished their conversation. It is with regret that my behaviour had deteriorated enough to cause comment. I now take special notice of these things and try to eliminate them. I know I do lapse into bad behaviour sometimes. There must be courtesy and respect, even in a heated debate.

I also found that there were issues when we had to toe the party line. This was a challenge for me. Especially when there was a conflict between protecting the environment and financial gain. Indeed, there were some who did not support me and labelled me a "greenie" and said that I should be in the Democrats party. Not helpful.

I was so relieved that whenever there was a controversial topic we were allowed to vote according to our conscience. This was the case when we were voting for the pokies, as to whether gambling machines should be allowed in clubs and pubs. The debate on this topic lasted until the small hours of the morning, and the legislation was won by one vote cast by a member of the Labor Party. I voted against the pokies legislation, as I had experience with my elder brother's gambling addiction, and had seen the results, when he lost the family's hard-earned fortune.

I kept communicating with groups that I had previous relations with—particularly women—so as to engender a closer relationship between people of diverse cultural backgrounds, and to try to interest other women in becoming politically active. These groups, formed while I was in parliament, were aimed at elevating the image of the Asian community, and Asian women in particular. Some of them were:

- Asian women colleagues and friends formed a group named 'Women of Diverse Cultural Backgrounds'. This group, apart from forming a social group to celebrate cultural festivals, hosted workshops exploring issues such as finances for home ownership for women, senior women's retirement plans, and women's health. I formed this group, and it is still in existence.
- Regular Asian Leaders' group meetings to discuss issues they were concerned with, in particular disadvantages due to race and customs, and to raise these issues to the relevant minister.
- The Asian and Mediterranean Food Festival group, where I coordinated a food festival of different cuisines, including Chinese, Indian, Greek and Italian. The Asian culture is to socialise over food, and the attempt was to show that the Liberal Party included migrants from many different countries of birth.

I also reached out as a medical graduate to the AMA (Australian Medical Association), and a visit was made to ask them about medical issues—and to perhaps form an easy conduit if there were political problems. The aim was to bring any significant issues to the attention of our health minister. This conduit was not used.

Even this visit was looked upon with a question mark as to whether I was trying to promote myself.

I was finally given something that I could do without raising eyebrows. I was appointed to chair a parliamentary sub-committee, the Social Development Committee—a standing committee. Two topics were raised for investigation. They were prostitution and poker machines in gambling—both controversial issues. I think that I was not pragmatic enough in the final write up, and identified that I was supportive of legalising prostitution and banning the use of poker machines in pubs and clubs.

MEMBERS AND OFFICERS OF
THE UNIVERSITY OF ADELAIDE COUNCIL, FEBRUARY 1996

BACK ROW: Mr HR Hassan, Mr TJ Kleinig, Mr SE Matthews [Minute Secretary], Prof FA Smith, Mr DJ Williams, Mr MC Stock, Mr IJ Bettison, Prof IR Falconer [Deputy Vice-Chancellor (Academic)], Mr BP Webb, The Hon Justice JW Perry, Dr SC Milazzo, Prof WD Williams, Dr PM Gill, Mr MR Buckby.

MIDDLE ROW: Mr DG McKie [Head, Secretariat], The Hon Ms JAW Levy, The Hon Dr BSL Pfitzner, Mr SNM Dullaway, Ms EA Summerfield, Prof AW Thomas, Mr FJ O'Neill [Registrar], Dr JTB Linn, Prof M O'Kane [Deputy Vice-Chancellor (Research)], Mr JF Keeler, Dr BC Teague

With former Premier of South Australia, Dean Brown.

47th Parliament, 1992

wasn't political enough, that I was too direct, and should have been more pragmatic. However, I note that now we have two Members of Parliament of Asian origin, whilst there were none when I arrived. Perhaps I have broken the glass ceiling.

As I journey, I have frequently felt physically alone. However, suddenly, I realise that I am surrounded by the sound of beautiful and harmonious chords coming from my immediate family and long-time friends.

From my two ex- husbands:

John: "Life is too short to dwell on regrets. Just package them away and enjoy the sunshine."

Oday: "You taught me to never give-up, and all I have is yours to have."

From Lian, my daughter: "Your book is fantastic."

From Christina, my close friend: "You inspire us. Thank you."

From Rob, my son: "Where are your family skeletons you told me about? Just sock it to them."

From Scarlett, my granddaughter: "I'm taller than you. We all can see it."

With all those sweet tones swirling around, how can I be alone?

www.ingramcontent.com/pod-product-compliance
Lightning Source LLC
LaVergne TN
LVHW052255070426
835507LV00035B/2918